**AMERICAN SCHOOL OF
NEEDLEWORK**

PRESENTS

The Great CHRISTMAS Craft Book

President: Jean Leinhauser
Director of Marketing and Book Coordinator: Rita Weiss
Project Coordinator, Knit and Crochet: Mary Thomas
Project Coordinator, Stitchery: Meredith Montross
Art Director: Carol Wilson Mansfield

Color Photography by Stemo Photography, Inc., Northbrook, Illinois
Roderick A. Stemo, President
James E. Zorn, Photographer

Book Design by CBG Graphics, Hartsdale, New York
Carol Belanger Grafton, Designer

S **STERLING PUBLISHING CO., NEW YORK**

We have made every effort to ensure the accuracy and
completeness of the instructions in this book.
We cannot, however, be responsible for human error,
typographical mistakes or variations in individual work.

Copyright © 1983 by the American School of Needlework, Inc.
Published by Sterling Publishing Co., Inc.
Two Park Avenue, New York, N.Y. 10016
Available in Canada from Oak Tree Press, Ltd.
c/o Canadian Manda Group, 215 Lakeshore Boulevard East,
Toronto, Ontario M5A 3W9

Introduction

For crafters—such as our staff at the American School of Needlework—Christmas is the highlight of the year!

Just as soon as the last bits of tinsel and evergreen needles are swept off the carpet, we are busy planning our creative projects for the next year.

In this book we have assembled for you a collection of our favorite Christmas projects. There are designs here to decorate your home and tree, to give as gifts, or to make and sell at the next bazaar.

You'll find projects in old-favorite skills—knitting, crocheting, patchwork—and we hope you will be tempted to try some of the newly popular techniques, such as counted cross stitch, candlewicking and needlepoint on plastic canvas. We've included complete step-by-step instructions on working each skill.

There is a special joy in giving when you share a part of yourself with a handmade project. We hope you will enjoy being Santa's Helper with the designs we have presented here.

A merry and "crafty" Christmas to all.

Jean Leinhauser

Jean Leinhauser
President
American School of Needlework, Inc.
3681 Commercial Avenue
Northbrook, Illinois 60062

ACKNOWLEDGMENTS

Several designs in this book were originally created by us for Coats & Clark, Inc., Stamford, Connecticut, and were copyrighted by them. It is with their kind permission that we are able to include those designs in this book.

To ensure the accuracy and clarity of our instructions, all of the projects in this book were tested by a group of dedicated and hard-working women, who made the designs which we have photographed. We express our appreciation to the following group of pattern testers:

Beverly Cartwright, Lincolnshire, Illinois
Almeda Colby, Northbrook, Illinois
Judy Demain, Highland Park, Illinois
Kim Hubal, Evanston, Illinois
Marilyn Kleinhardt, Northbrook, Illinois
Joan Kokaska, Wildwood, Illinois
Marjorie McGowan, Evanston, Illinois
Margaret Miller, Chicago, Illinois
Karen Moe, Buffalo Grove, Illinois
Meredith Montross, Wilmette, Illinois
Wanda Parker, Mundelein, Illinois
Judy Shambrook, Lincolnshire, Illinois
Anita Simes, Northbrook, Illinois
Addie Snett, Northbrook, Illinois
Rosemarie Stanley, Park Ridge, Illinois
Diane Streicker, Wilmette, Illinois
Shirley Sutscheck, Park Ridge, Illinois
Mary Thomas, Libertyville, Illinois
Gretchen Wilhelm, Chicago, Illinois
Mary Ellen Wyld, Morton Grove, Illinois

We also acknowledge our thanks and appreciation to the following contributing designers:

Judy Demain, Highland Park, Illinois
Anis Duncan, Northbrook, Illinois
Solveig Carlson, Glencoe, Illinois
Don FranzMeier, Wheeling, Illinois
Louise O'Donnell, Boulder, Colorado
Sue Penrod, Loveland, Colorado
Carol Wilson Mansfield, Northbrook, Illinois
Julie A. Ryan, Highland Park, Illinois
Anita Simes, Northbrook, Illinois
Mary Thomas, Libertyville, Illinois
Rita Weiss, Pound Ridge, New York
Gretchen Wilhelm, Chicago, Illinois

Contents

PATCHWORK   7

Patchwork How-To   8
Christmas Pillows   13
Christmas Trees Placemats and Napkins   19
Christmas Tote Bag   21
Christmas Stocking   23
Spinning Triangles Tree Skirt   25

POMPONS   27

Pompon How-To   28
Pompon Santa   30
Pompon Christmas Tree   31

PLASTIC CANVAS NEEDLEPOINT   33

Plastic Canvas How-To   34
Christmas Placemat, Coaster and Napkin Ring   37
Little Trunk Gift Box   40
The Little Log Cabin in the Woods   42
Christmas Cottage   46
Santa Centerpiece   51
Christmas Party Table Decorations   54
Christmas Church   61

COLOR PLATES   65–80

COUNTED CROSS STITCH   81

Counted Cross Stitch How-To   82
Nativity Grouping   86
Christmas Tree Stocking   91
Christmas Tree with Dimensional Ornaments   94
Christmas Angel Ornaments   96
Christmas Around the World Wall Hanging   97
Nativity Set   100
Mr. and Mrs. Claus Ornaments   104

CROCHETING & KNITTING   105

Crocheting and Knitting How-To   106
Little Tree-Top Angel   113
Mini Christmas Stockings   115
Crocheted Snowflakes   117
Crocheted Pineapple Ornament   119
Crocheted Christmas Table Tree   121
Jingle Tree Christmas Decoration   123
Christmas Stockings   125

CANDLEWICKING   133

Candlewicking How-To   134
Candlewick Christmas Tree Ornaments   136
Candlewick Snowflakes   138
Candlewick Mini Christmas Wreaths   141
Candlewick Tree-Top Angels   142

INDEX   144

PATCHWORK

The old-fashioned craft of patchwork truly expresses the warmth and homey comfort of the season. Whether you're an old-hand at patchwork, or if you've just begun to work with this fascinating technique, you're sure to find something in this chapter that will make your Christmas season brighter.

PATCHWORK HOW-TO

TEMPLATES

All of the pattern shapes used in making these projects are given in actual-size templates on pages 11, 12. Each project will indicate which templates are to be used for that project. Carefully trace the template shapes onto heavy cardboard, such as a medium-weight illustration board, and cut them out. (Special plastic for making templates is also available in quilt shops or departments.)

The templates are designed to be used for either machine or hand piecing. If you are planning to piece your blocks by machine, cut out the template on the broken line to include the ¼" seam allowance. If you are planning to piece your block by hand, cut out the template on the solid line.

It is important that all templates be cut carefully because if they are not accurate, the patchwork will not fit together. Use a pair of good-size sharp scissors, a single-edged razor blade or an X-Acto knife. Be careful not to bend the corners of the triangles.

FABRICS

All of our fabric requirements are based upon 44"-45" wide fabrics. If you use other widths, be sure you adjust fabric requirements accordingly.

Old-time quilts were traditionally made of 100% cotton, and this is still the fabric that most experienced patchworkers prefer. It is easy to work with and will wear much better than almost any other type of fabric. If you have difficulty locating 100% cotton, you can use a blend, but try not to use anything with more than approximately 30% synthetic. The fabric should be soft and fairly closely woven so that the seams will hold and the edges will not fray easily when cut. Be careful, however, of fabrics that are so closely woven that you will have difficulty pushing the needle through them. Avoid fabrics that have been treated with a finish since they are difficult to work with.

We have specified colors for the various projects, but feel free to experiment with your own color choices. Color is such a matter of personal preference that it is difficult to set up any hard and fast rules. If you like certain color combinations, they are correct for you! Be free and creative, using your own intuitive color sense. Just remember that you should not use prints that are so large that the entire print cannot appear in the smallest patchwork piece.

Before you begin your project, wash all fabric to check that it is colorfast and pre-shrunk (don't trust those manufacturers' labels). Test for colorfastness by washing in fairly hot water; be especially careful of dark reds and dark greens which can bleed if the initial dyeing was not carefully done.

CUTTING THE FABRIC

Cutting the patchwork pieces is one of the most important steps in making a professional-looking patchwork project. In order to have the pieces fit, you have to be accurate.

First iron your pre-washed fabric to remove any creases or wrinkles. The grain line of the fabric should be checked carefully. Lengthwise threads should be parallel to the selvage and crosswise threads perpendicular to the selvage as in *Fig 1* to insure that the fabric is straight so that the pieces will be cut correctly. If a fabric is off-grain, you can straighten it. Pull gently on the true bias in the opposite direction to the off-grain edge as in *Fig 2*. Continue doing this until the crosswise threads are at a right angle to the lengthwise threads. Lay your freshly ironed fabric on a large, smooth surface with the wrong side up.

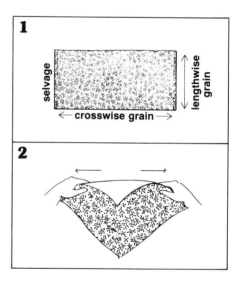

CUTTING FOR MACHINE SEWING: Lay the cardboard template (cut on the broken line) on the wrong side of the fabric near the top left edge of the material (but not on the selvage), placing it so that as many straight sides of the piece as possible are parallel to the crosswise and lengthwise grain of the fabric (*Fig 3*). Try to keep the long side of the triangles on the true bias by placing the short sides of the triangles on the straight of the fabric. Diamonds should be placed so that two sides of the diamond are on the straight of the fabric (two will be on the bias). Trace around the template. You can mark with a regular well-sharpened, hard lead pencil, or a white or light blue dressmaker's pencil for dark fabrics. Many quilt makers like to use fabric marking pens, architect's pencils, ballpoint pens, etc. Test any marking material to make certain that it will not run when wet. There are a number of cold water-soluble quilt marking pens

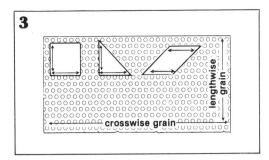

currently on the market. These pens can be used to mark both the backs and fronts of fabric so that you can use them later for marking quilting designs. Cold water is supposed to make these markings disappear, but once again never trust the manufacturer's label. Always test everything just to be sure.

Continue moving the template and tracing it on the fabric the required number of times, moving from left to right and always keeping the straight lines parallel to the grain. If you wish to save fabric, have the pieces share a common cutting line as in *Fig 4*.

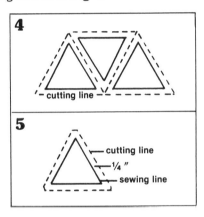

CUTTING FOR HAND SEWING: Lay the cardboard template (cut on the solid line) on the fabric as described above for machine piecing, and trace around it with your marking tool. Now measure ¼″ around this shape. Using a ruler, draw this second line. This is the cutting line (*Fig 5*). The first line (where you traced your template) is your stitching line. The seam allowance does not have to be perfect because it will not show. The sewing line, however, must be perfectly straight or the pieces will not fit together into a perfectly shaped design. You may discover that you don't actually have to draw this second line with a ruler; your eye can become so accustomed to the ¼″ seam allowance that you will be able to determine it without the ruler.

SEWING THE PATCHWORK PIECES

Before starting to sew, make sure that you will be working with well-ironed fabric. If your pieces have been sitting in your sewing basket for several days and are wrinkled, iron them carefully before beginning to sew.

SEWING THE PATCHWORK BY HAND: Place two pieces together with right sides facing and place a pin through both pieces at each end of the pencil line (*Fig 6*).

Check on the back to make sure that the pins are exactly on the pencil lines. When sewing large seams, place pins every 1½″, removing the pins as you sew past them. Always stitch on the sewing line, being very careful not to stitch into the margins at the corners (*Fig 7*). Use a fairly short needle (#7 to #10) and no more than an 18″ length of thread. Join the pieces with short, simple running stitches, taking a few back stitches at the beginning and end of each seam rather than a knot. If the seam is very long, make a few back stitches at various places along the seam. When you sew two bias edges together (as in sewing two triangles along the long side), try to keep the thread taut enough so that the edges do not stretch as you sew them.

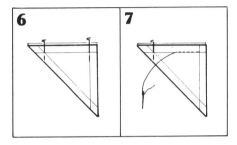

After you join the pieces, iron the seams flat to one side, not open. Generally, seams can all be ironed in the same direction, but darker pieces should be ironed so that they do not fall under lighter pieces since they may show through when the patchwork is completed. You can turn the seam on top in one direction and the seam on the bottom in the opposite direction as in *Fig 8*. This will keep seams that are crossed with other seams from bunching at the crossing points. Clip away excess fabric at these points if necessary. All seams should be ironed before they are crossed with another seam.

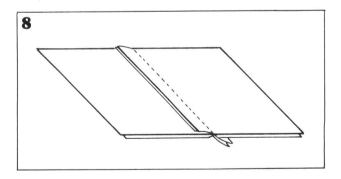

SEWING THE PATCHWORK BY MACHINE: Place the two pieces together with right sides facing and the top edges even. Set the sewing machine for about 10 stitches to the inch and use a size 14 needle. Machine piecing is best done with the straight-stitch foot and throat plate on the machine. Measure ¼″ from your needle hole to the right side of the presser foot and place a piece of tape on the plate. Keep the edge of your piece lined up with this marking, and you will be able to sew with a perfect ¼″ seam line. Follow the basic instructions for sewing the pieces together by hand: pin the seam, baste (if desired)

and sew. Be careful that you do not sew over pins even if your machine permits this. Sewing over pins tends to weaken the seam. When crossing seams, be especially careful to match seam to seam. It helps if the lower seam is turned one way and the top seam the other. After you have joined the pieces, iron the seams as described for hand sewing.

BLOCKING

Most patchwork will require some "blocking" after the work has been completed. The term "blocking" means keeping the edges straight on all sides so that the finished piece will be a perfect rectangle. If your project is made with more than one square, block each square separately, and then give the entire piece a final blocking when all of the squares have been joined.

Pad the surface of your ironing board with an old terry towel. Place the completed patchwork face down on the terry towel, and pull the edges straight. Place rust-proof pins at the corners and along all sides to hold the piece in shape. Cover the patchwork with a damp cloth, and steam it lightly (or use a steam iron). Do not touch the iron to the cloth or back of the patchwork—let the steam do the work. Steam the edges until they are perfectly square and of equal measurements. Steam the center last. The patchwork should be flat and free of puckers.

QUILTING

Most of the projects in this book require some simple quilting, and—like a quilt—consist of three parts: the top, the filler or batting, and the backing. Most of the quilting consists of outlining around the patchwork pieces, and these quilting lines do not need to be marked on the top. However, you may wish to mark some of the other suggested quilting patterns—such as the quilting lines on the placemat—before the completed patchwork is joined to the batting and the backing. Mark all quilting lines on the right side of the fabric. There are a number of methods for marking on the fabric, but test any to make certain that it will wash out. One of the easiest is simply to use a hard lead pencil. If the fabric is dark, try chalk or a piece of white soap, trimmed to a thin point. If you sew directly on the pencil or chalk lines, the lines probably will not show when the work is finished. You might also want to experiment with some of the new water-soluble marking pens discussed earlier. The best advice is to test all of these marking materials first to find the one that works the best for you.

Lay your backing, wrong side up, on a large flat surface. To keep the corners from moving, you might want to secure them with pins, tacks or masking tape. Spread the batting over the backing, making sure that there are no lumps or thin spots. Pin both layers together, and then fasten the batting to the backing with long basting stitches. Start in the center and sew toward the edges with large stitches in a number of diagonal lines. Be sure that your knots are on the outside of the backing fabric and use a thread color which will be easy to detect when you are ready to remove the basting threads. Now lay the completed patchwork in place over the backing and the batting. Pin this in place and baste the three layers as you basted the first two. Keep basting stitches no more than 6″ apart.

Most of the projects in this chapter can be quilted quite satisfactorily in an embroidery hoop or a small quilting frame. Place the hoop over the center of the patchwork, pulling the patchwork slightly taut (not as tight as for embroidery) and moving any extra fullness toward the edges. Always begin working in the center of the patchwork and quilt toward the outside edges. Quilting stitches have a tendency to push the batting, and by quilting from the center out you can gradually ease any excess fullness toward the edges rather than finding a big lump in the center of the work. Small projects can often be quilted without the use of a hoop or frame. Just be sure that the three layers are basted together quite securely before you begin to sew.

The actual quilting stitch is a fairly easy one for anyone who has ever sewn. It is just a very simple running stitch, but getting that stitch through three thicknesses may take some practice. Use one of the short, fine needles especially designed for quilting (they are called "betweens"). Try to use the shortest possible needle because shorter needles usually mean shorter stitches. The preferred thread for quilting is a 100% cotton thread, but if you are unable to locate it, you can use a strong (#50 or #30) mercerized cotton or cotton-coated polyester. To keep thread from tangling, run it through a cake of beeswax before you start.

Begin with an 18″ piece of quilting thread with a knot in one end. Go into the quilt through the top approximately ½″ from where you are planning to begin your quilting, and bring your needle up to the quilting line. Pull gently but firmly and the knot will slip through the top layer into the padding where it will not be seen. Try making the stitches as close together as you can; this is the real secret of fine quilting. Expert quilters insist that quilting stitches should be no less than five to ten per inch. Don't be discouraged, however, if your stitches are longer. It is more important that the stitches be evenly spaced so that they are the same length on the front as on the back. Don't quilt over the basting stitches; they will become impossible to remove. To finish off a thread, make a single back stitch and run the thread through the batting. Cut. The end will be lost!

PATCHWORK TEMPLATES

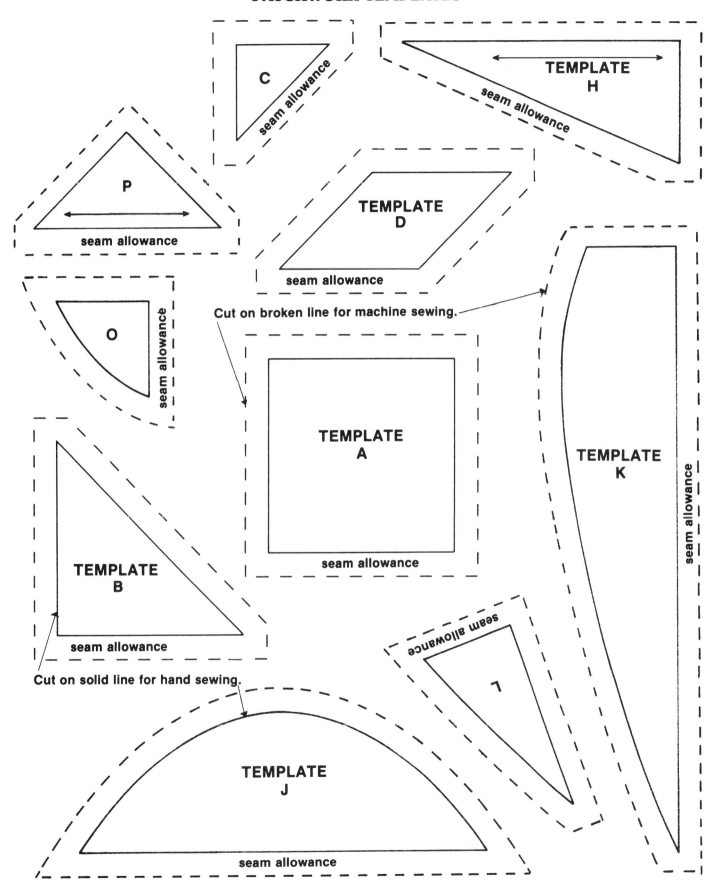

11

PATCHWORK TEMPLATES

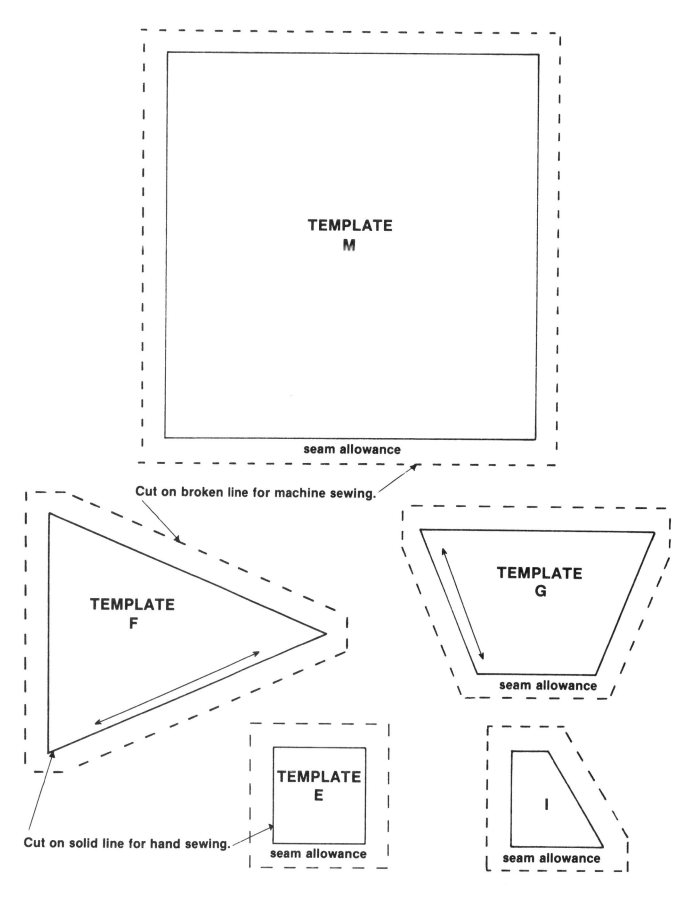

TEMPLATE
M

seam allowance

Cut on broken line for machine sewing.

TEMPLATE
F

TEMPLATE
G

seam allowance

Cut on solid line for hand sewing.

TEMPLATE
E

seam allowance

I

seam allowance

12

CHRISTMAS PILLOWS

designed by Rita Weiss

A patchwork pillow is a wonderful introduction to the world of patchwork quilt-making because it contains all of the elements of a full-size quilt (patchwork top, batting, backing), but in miniature. Basically all patchwork pillows—no matter their size—are made in the same manner. The patchwork is completed and basted to the backing and batting. Because the backing does not show, it is usually made of unbleached muslin rather than a matching fabric. Then the "miniature quilt" is quilted through the backing and the batting. If your quilting stitches are not too expert on the back, this will not show in a pillow; so it's a good project for practicing quilting skills! Here are step-by-step instructions for making a pillow.

Making a Knife Edge Pillow

Step 1: Complete the patchwork according to the instructions.

Step 2: Measure the completed patchwork and cut a piece of batting about 1″ larger all around.

Step 3: Cut a piece of unbleached muslin to the same size as the batting.

Step 4: Join the three pieces following the directions given in the Patchwork How-To for a regular patchwork project. Quilt. Cut the batting and the backing even with the top.

Step 5: If piping is desired, purchase ready-made piping in a matching or contrasting color. You can make your own piping by folding a bias strip around cording. Sew by hand or with the zipper or cording foot on the sewing machine. Place the completed piping along the sides of the pillow with raw edges even. Baste the piping along the ¼″ seam allowance.

Step 6: If a ruffle is desired, make your own from the fabric or purchase pre-gathered ruffling. Pre-gathered trimming will require the total measurement of all four sides of the pillow plus an additional ½″ for the overlaps where the edges meet. If you are making your own ruffling, figure on double the measurements of the four sides plus an extra 2″ for overlap. To make your own ruffle, cut a long strip and join the two ends of the strip at the shorter edges to make a circle. Wrong sides together, fold the circle in half lengthwise and iron down the crease. By machine or hand make one or two rows of gathering stitches ¼″ in from the raw edge through both pieces of fabric. Carefully pull up the threads to gather the ruffle until it is the proper size.

Step 7: Baste the ruffle in place on the *right* side of the patchwork as in *Fig 1*.

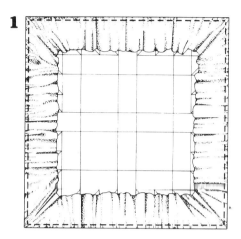

Step 8: Now measure your completed patchwork and cut the pillow backing fabric the same size as the completed top.

Step 9: With right sides together, pin the sides leaving a large enough opening at one of the sides to comfortably turn the entire piece right side out.

Step 10: Stitch around the sides; be especially careful not to get any of the patchwork design or the ruffling caught in the stitching. Work for slightly rounded corners, even though the design is perfectly square. Very pointed corners are difficult to turn and stuff.

Step 11: Turn the pillow right side out and check to make sure that none of the patchwork design is obscured by the stitching and that everything is to your liking. Now turn the pillow back to the wrong side and clip slightly into the corners, being especially careful not to clip the stitches. Clip away any excess batting or fabric.

Step 12: Turn the pillow right side out. You can either stuff the pillow with polyester fiberfill or use a pillow form. (Be sure to get the fiber into corners.) If you are planning to use a pillow form, be sure to leave a slightly larger opening for inserting the pillow form.

Step 13: When the pillow is completely stuffed, turn under the unfinished edge and slip stitch in place.

Hint: The four corners of prefinished pillow forms are often not filled properly. To create a really plump pillow, open the pillow form at the four corners and insert additional fiber fill.

Making a Box Pillow

Step 1: Follow steps 1–8 under "Making a Knife Edge Pillow".

Step 2: Carefully measure the four sides of the com-

pleted pillow top and cut a side strip which is that measurement (plus an additional ½″ for seam allowances).

Step 3: With right sides together, pin around the patchwork top and the side strip. Stitch around, being careful not to get any of the patchwork design caught in the stitching. Work for slightly rounded corners, even though the design is perfectly square. Very pointed corners are difficult to turn and stuff.

Step 4: With right sides together, pin the pillow backing to the strip, leaving a large enough opening at one of the sides to comfortably turn the entire piece right side out.

Step 5: Stitch around the sides as described in Step 3, but leaving the opening.

Step 6: Follow steps 11–13 under "Making a Knife Edge Pillow".

STAR OF BETHLEHEM PILLOW

Size
Approximately 20″ × 20″

Materials
¼ yard green print
¼ yard dk red print
¼ yard lt red print
1¼ yards white (*includes pillow backing*)
22″ × 22″ pieces of unbleached muslin and batting
Polyester fiber fill or foam cut to size
2½ yds narrow cording

Templates
A, B, C, D and E

Instructions
Step 1: Cut the following:
Template A: 24 white
Template B: 16 white
Template C: 32 white, 16 green print, 24 dk red print, 24 lt red print

Template D: 48 dk red print, 40 green print, 40 lt red print
Template E: 32 white

2

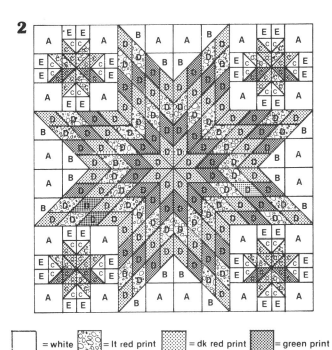

☐ = white   ◌ = lt red print   ▦ = dk red print   ▨ = green print

Step 2: Following *Fig 2*, make patchwork. It will be easier if you work in four quarters. Start with upper left; then work upper right. Join these two sections. Now make the lower left and the lower right and join these two sections. Join both of these sections with one long seam in the middle.

Step 3: Complete pillow, following the instructions on page 13 for making a knife-edged pillow with piping, and quilting according to *Fig 3*.

3

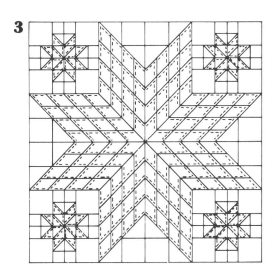

BROKEN STAR PILLOW

Size
Approximately 16″ × 16″

Materials
¾ yard red pin dot (*includes backing*)
¼ yard each, white print and green print
18″ × 18″ pieces of unbleached muslin and batting
Polyester fiber fill or pillow form
2 yds narrow cording

Templates
A and B

Instructions
Step 1: Cut the following:
Template A: 4 white
Template B: 44 white, 40 red, 36 green

Step 2: Following *Fig 4*, make the patchwork.

4

(white) B	(red) B	(white) B B	(white) B	(white) B B	(white) B	(red) B B	(white) B
(green)	(white)	(green)	(red)	(green)	(red)	(white)	(green)
(red) B	(red) B B	(green) B B	(red) B	(green) B B	(red) B	(green) B B	(red) B
(white)	(green)	(white)	(red)	(white)	(white)	(red)	(white)
(red) B B	(green) B	**A** (white)	(white) B B	(white)	**A** (white)	(red) B B	(white) B
(white)	(red)		(red)	(green)		(green)	(white)
(white) B	(green) B B	(green) B	(red) B B	(green) B	(red) B	(red) B	(white) B B
(green)	(white)	(white)	(green)	(red)	(green)	(red)	(green)
(red) B B	(white) B	(white) B	(red) B B	(green) B	(green) B B	(white) B B	(green) B
(white)	(red)	(red)	(green)	(red)	(green)	(green)	(white)
(white) B	(green) B B	**A** (white)	(green)	(red)	**A** (white)	(red) B B	(white) B
(green)	(red)		(white)	(white)		(green)	(red)
(white) B B	(red) B	(green) B B	(white) B	(red) B B	(white) B	(white) B B	(white) B
(red)	(green)	(red)	(green)	(green)	(red)	(red)	(red)
(green) B B	(white) B	(red) B B	(green) B	(red) B B	(green) B	(white) B B	(green) B
(white)	(red)	(white)	(white)	(red)	(white)	(red)	(white)

15

5

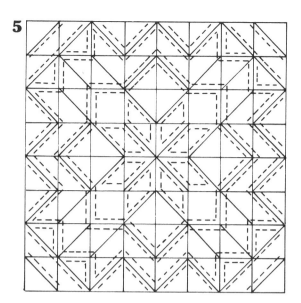

Step 3: Complete pillow, following the instructions on page 13 for making a knife-edged pillow with piping, and quilting according to *Fig 5*.

POINSETTIA PILLOW

Size
Approximately 16″ × 16″

Materials
1¼ yards green dot (*includes backing and piping*)
10″ × 10″ piece gold
12″ × 12″ piece red print
¼ yard red
18″ × 18″ pieces of unbleached muslin and batting
2 yds narrow cording
Polyester fiber fill or pillow form

Templates
A, B, C, M and P

Instructions
Step 1: Cut the following:
Template A: 8 green dot, 1 gold, 8 red
Template B: 20 green dot, 16 red, 12 red print
Template C: 28 gold, 4 red print
Template M: 4 green dot
Template P: 8 red print, 4 gold

Step 2: Following *Fig 6*, make the patchwork.

6

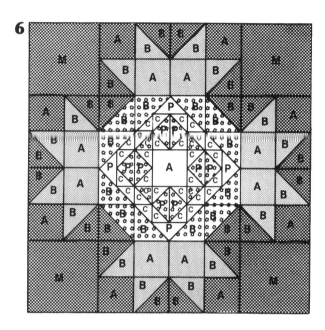

▨ = green dot   ▦ = red print   ▧ = red   ☐ = gold

7

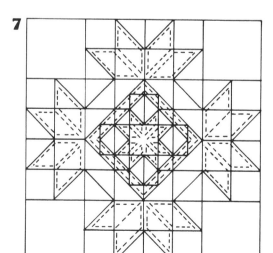

Step 3: Complete pillow, following the instructions on page 13 for making a knife-edged pillow with piping, and quilting according to *Fig 7*.

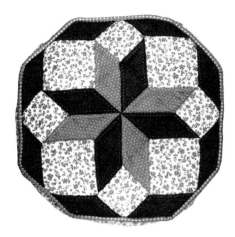

ROLLING STAR PILLOW

Size

Approximately 12″ in diameter

Materials

½ yard white print (*includes borders and backing*)
¼ yard green
¼ yard red pin dot (*includes piping*)
14″ × 14″ pieces of unbleached muslin and batting
2¼ yards narrow cording
Polyester fiber fill

Templates

A and B

Instructions

Step 1: Cut the following:
Template A: 4 white print
Template B: 24 green, 16 white print, 8 red pin dot

Step 2: Following *Fig 8*, make the patchwork.

Step 3: Complete pillow, following the instructions on page 14 for making a box pillow with piping, and quilting according to *Fig 9*.

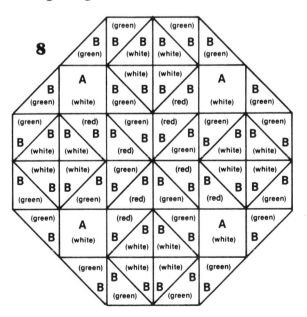

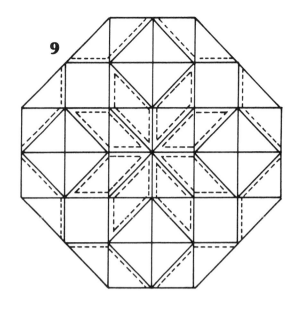

CHRISTMAS STAR PILLOW

Size

Approximately 20″ × 20″

Materials

⅓ yard white
Small pieces (*approximately 15″ × 15″*) red stripe, green and green print
¾ yard red pin dot (*includes piping and backing*)
22″ × 22″ pieces of unbleached muslin and batting
2⅓ yards narrow cording
Polyester fiber fill or pillow form

Templates

A and B

Instructions

Step 1: Cut the following:
Template A: 28 white, 4 green, 4 red stripe, 4 green print

Template B: 32 white, 24 green, 24 red stripe [we reversed the stripe on half the pieces], 24 green print, 16 red pin dot

Step 2: Following *Fig 10*, make the patchwork. It will be easier if you work in four quarters. Start with the upper left; then work the upper right. Join these two sections. Now make the lower left and the lower right and join these two sections. Join both of these sections together with one long seam in the middle.

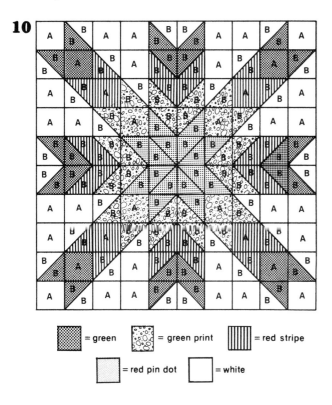

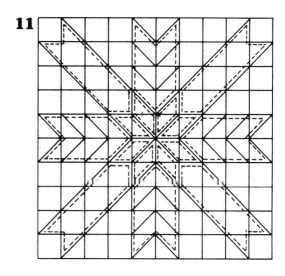

= green   = green print   = red stripe

= red pin dot   = white

Step 3: Complete pillow, following the instructions on page 13 for making a knife-edged pillow with piping, and quilting according to *Fig 11*.

CHRISTMAS TREES
PLACEMATS AND NAPKINS

designed by Rita Weiss

Set your Christmas table with this cheery set of Christmas placemats and napkins, and your guests are sure to start a round of "Jingle Bells." The materials listed will make four placemats and four napkins. If the quilting is done very carefully, the placemats will be reversible.

Size

Placemats, approximately 13″ × 17″
Napkins, approximately 14″ × 14″

Materials

¾ yard green print (*includes two napkins*)
¾ yard white print (*includes two napkins*)
2 yards red (*includes backing*)
¾ yard batting

Templates

F and H

PLACEMAT

Instructions

Step 1: Cut the following for *each* placemat:
Template F: 9 green print; 9 white print; 12 red
Template H: 12 red
Center piece, 12½″ × 7″: 1 red (see Step 3 before cutting)

Step 2: Following *Fig 1*, make the bottom, top strips and two side strips of patchwork.

Step 3: Measure the patchwork pieces and carefully cut your center piece to fit. Be sure to allow the ¼″ seam allowance all around.

Step 4: Attach the two side pieces of patchwork to the center piece and then join the top and bottom pieces.

Step 5: Measure the placemat and cut the batting and backing the same size. Right sides together, baste the placemat to the backing; baste the batting to the wrong side of the placemat.

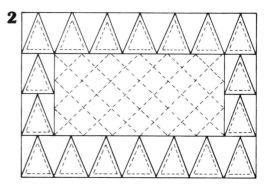

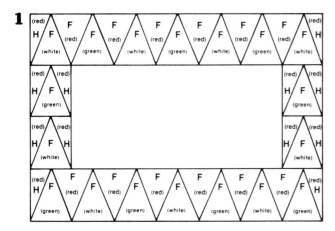

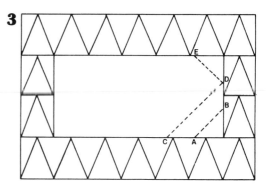

Step 6: Stitch around the ¼″ seam allowance, leaving a large enough opening for turning. Trim all of the layers even; remove the basting stitches, turn and slip stitch the opening. (*NOTE: If you are joining by machine, try placing some tissue paper under the batting so that the batting does not get caught as you work. Tear the tissue paper away when you have finished joining the seam.*)

Step 7: Quilt, following the suggested quilting design in *Fig 2*. To make the diagonal quilting lines along the middle piece, begin at the lower right hand corner of the middle section and measure 2″ up from the bottom (see *Fig 3*). Make a small mark (A). Make another similar mark along the bottom of the middle section 2″ in from the right hand corner (B). Join these two marks with a diagonal line (AB). Starting at this bottom diagonal line, make diagonal lines 2″ apart (measuring from mark A) from the bottom right of the middle section to the top left (C-D, etc.). Using this same technique, draw intersecting diagonal lines across the middle section from the top right to the bottom left (E-F, etc.). The intersections will make the diamond shaped quilting pattern. This is a miniature

version of the old quilt marking technique called "Snapping the String." Always remember to quilt from the center out.

NAPKINS

Instructions

Step 1: Cut the following:
Square, 15″ × 15″: 2 green print, 2 white print

Step 2: Turn under ¼″ all around, and hem by hand or machine.

CHRISTMAS TOTE BAG

designed by Rita Weiss

Make this tote bag early in the season in bright Christmas colors; then use it to carry home your Christmas presents.

Size

Approximately 12″ × 12″ × 6″

Materials

¼ yard white
⅓ yard red print
¾ yard green print
½ yard green (*for lining*)
¾ yard each unbleached muslin and batting
3 yards narrow cording

Templates

A and B

Instructions

Step 1: Cut the following:
Template A: 8 white

Template B: 16 each of white, red print, and green print
Border strips, 2½″ × 8½″: 4 white (for top and bottom)
Border strips, 2½″ × 12½″: 4 green print (for sides)
Side strip, 6½″ × 37½″: 1 green print (see Step 8 before cutting)
Straps, 3½″ × 12½″: 2 green print, 2 red print
Bias strip, 1½″ × 37½″: 2 red print
Lining, 12½″ × 12½″: 2 green
      6½″ × 37½″: 1 green (see Step 8 before cutting)
Backing, 12½″ × 12½″: 2 muslin
Filling, 12½″ × 12½″: 2 batting

Step 2: Following *Fig 1*, make two patchwork blocks.

Step 3: Attach the top, bottom and side strips to each block as in *Fig 2*.

Step 4: Baste the batting to the muslin; then place the patchwork on top of the batting and baste through all three thicknesses.

Step 5: Quilt, following the suggested quilting lines in *Fig 3*.

1

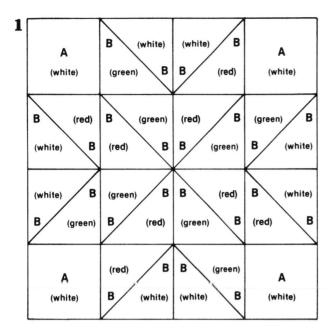

A (white)	**B** (white) (green) **B**	**B** (white) **B** (red)	**A** (white)
B (red) (white) **B**	**B** (green) (red) **B**	**B** (red) **B** (green)	**B** (green) **B** (white)
B (white) (green) **B**	**B** (green) (red) **B**	**B** (red) **B** (green)	**B** (white) **B** (red)
A (white)	(red) **B** **B** (white)	**B** (green) **B** (white)	**A** (white)

2

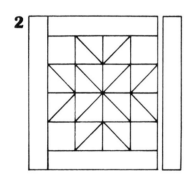

3

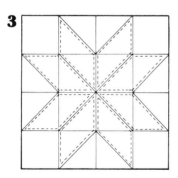

4

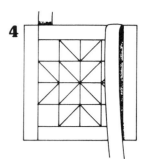

Step 6: Make the straps by pinning red print and green print right sides together. Using the ¼″ seam allowance, sew three sides together, leaving one short side for turning. Trim the corners and turn right side out. Repeat for second strap. Pin raw edges of the straps to the outside of the bag, matching green print to outside. One strap is attached to each side of the bag, and the two edges are approximately 3½″ apart (**Fig 4**).

Step 7: Make the piping by folding the red print bias strip around the narrow cording and sewing by hand or with the zipper or cording foot on the sewing machine. If you prefer you may use a ready-made cording in a matching or contrasting color. Place the completed piping along the sides and bottom of the patchwork with the raw edges even. Baste the piping along the ¼″ seam allowance. Repeat for the second piece.

Step 8: Measure the completed work and cut the side strip so that it is sufficiently long enough to go around the two sides and bottom. Be sure to include the seam allowance at the top.

Step 9: Right sides together, pin the side strip to the front of the bag and then sew the strip to the bottom and sides of the front of the bag. Carefully clip into the corners so that the bag will lie flat. Join the back of the bag to the side strip in the same manner. **Do not turn inside out.**

Step 10: Make the lining, following the directions given above in Steps 8 and 9. **Turn the lining right side out.**

Step 11: With the right sides together, place the lining into the bag, keeping the completed handles facing down. Match the seams. Carefully stitch along the ¼″ seam allowance across the top, leaving an opening large enough for turning. (Try to keep this opening away from the handles.) Turn inside out and tuck the lining into the bag. Fold under the remaining seam allowances and slip stitch the lining to the bag.

Step 12: Top stitch around the top of bag if desired. Tie straps as desired.

CHRISTMAS STOCKING

designed by Rita Weiss

Hang this stocking on your fireplace and Santa will have lots of room for goodies! While the stocking may look complicated to piece, it is really quite simple. It is constructed of three quilt blocks; one on the top and two on the bottom. The top is based upon the "Pine Tree" quilt block. The bottom boot section is made of two miniature "Windmill" blocks, with the small "O" template making the curve of the heel on one of the blocks and a piece made from the C template missing on the second block to achieve the curve at the instep. After the two blocks for the boot section are made, they are bordered with a strip of squares made from the E template plus the special I, J, K and L templates to achieve the proper shape. The materials listed below will make both sides of the stocking. If you make one side plain, simply divide the number of pieces in half and use your completed stocking to make a pattern for the second side. Adjust fabric requirements.

Size

Approximately 15″ long

Materials

½ yard red
Small pieces (*approximately 12″ × 12″*) of each of following: green print, green dot and brown
½ yard green stripe (*includes lining*)
½ yard each of unbleached muslin and batting

Templates

A, B, C, E, I, J, K, L, O and P

Instructions

Step 1: Cut the following:
Template A: 2 brown
Template B: 4 red
Template C: 64 green dot; 46 green print; 56 green stripe; 40 red; 16 brown
Template E: 28 red; 16 brown
Template I: 2 red
Template J: 2 red
Template K: 2 red
Template L: 2 red
Template O: 2 green print
Template P: 2 brown
Border strips, 1″ × 6½″: 4 red (for top and bottom)
Border strips, 1″ × 9½″: 4 red (for sides)

Step 2: Following *Fig 1*, construct the "Pine Tree" block, adding the borders. Then construct the boot section of the stocking; start by making the "Windmill" blocks, and then add the other pieces.

Step 3: Join the top and bottom sections together.

Step 4: Using the completed patchwork as a pattern, cut two stockings from the lining material.

Step 5: Cut a square of batting and a square of the

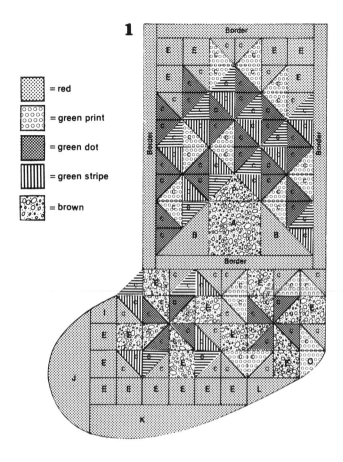

1

Border

Border

Border

Border

- ▨ = red
- ▨ = green print
- ▨ = green dot
- ▥ = green stripe
- ▨ = brown

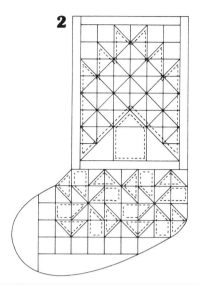

2

unbleached muslin approximately 2″ larger all around than the completed patchwork. Baste the batting to the backing following the directions on page 10. Lay the completed patchwork, right side up, on the backing and batting and carefully baste. Quilt the stocking, following **Fig 2**. Cut away the unused batting and backing.

Step 6: Repeat for the second side.

Step 7: Right sides together, join the two sides of the stocking, sewing down the sides and along the bottom of the foot. Clip where necessary to allow for the turn. **Do not turn the stocking right side out.**

Step 8: Right sides together, join the two lining pieces of the stocking, sewing down the sides and along the bottom of the foot. Clip where necessary to allow for the turning. **Turn right side out.**

Step 9: Right sides together, carefully place the lining into the stocking. Match the seams. Carefully stitch across the ¼″ seam allowance at the top of the stocking, leaving an opening large enough for turning. Turn right side out and tuck the lining into the stocking. Fold under the un-finished seam allowances and slip stitch the lining to the stocking.

SPINNING TRIANGLES TREE SKIRT

designed by Rita Weiss

This tree skirt is an enlarged version of the "Spinning Triangles" quilt block. Although this project may be time-consuming, it is not difficult. Small triangles are simply sewn together to form eight larger triangles, which are then joined to make the skirt. When joining triangles, try to sew a bias edge to a straight edge, rather than two bias edges together. If you wish to enlarge the skirt, add another row of triangles.

Size

Approximately 36″ in diameter

Materials

½ yard red
⅔ yard green
¾ yard print
40″ × 40″ pieces of batting and unbleached muslin

Templates

F and G

Instructions

Step 1: Cut the following:
Template F: 48 red, 72 green, 112 print
Template G: 4 red, 4 print

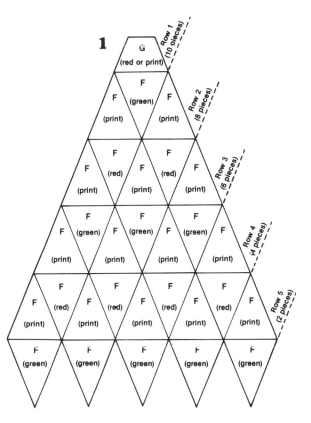

Step 2: Following *Fig 1* work in rows to construct the 8 large triangles. Four of the triangles will have a red piece cut from the G template and four will have a print piece cut from the G template.

Step 3: Join the triangles to each other, leaving the eighth seam open as in *Fig 2*.

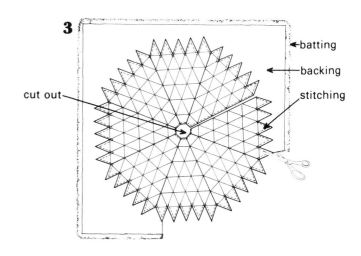

Step 7: Quilt, following the suggested quilting outline in *Fig 4*.

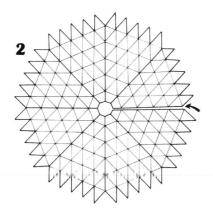

Step 4: Lay the square of batting (slightly larger than the completed patchwork) on a flat surface and cover with the unbleached muslin, right side up. Baste carefully. Lay the completed patchwork on the muslin, *wrong* side up and baste carefully.

Step 5: Carefully stitch around the outer edges as shown in *Fig 3*, leaving the eighth triangle seam open. Carefully cut away the excess fabric and batting. Clip into corners and trim. Turn right side out and push into the corners with a blunt pencil or similar tool. (*NOTE: If you are joining by machine, try placing some tissue paper under the batting so that the batting does not get caught as you work. Tear the tissue paper away when you have finished joining the seam.*)

Step 6: Slip stitch the opening.

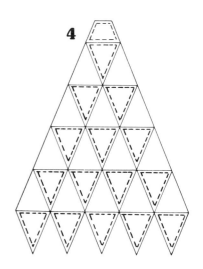

26

POMPONS

Pompon projects are easy and fun! It's really amazing what delightful creations you can make with bits of yarn, glue, felt, flowers and beads. Pompon projects not only make wonderful Christmas decorations, but are ideal for bazaars. Children can help, too, making these good family projects.

POMPON HOW-TO

The projects in this book can be constructed with either ready-made or hand-made pompons. Ready-made pompons are available in sizes from ¼″ to 3″ in diameter.

Hand-made and ready-made pompons can be combined in a project. For the tiny sizes, it is often easier to use a ready-made pompon. It is really a matter of personal choice as to which you use. Ready-made pompons are usually acrylic, and come in a wide variety of colors. They are tied in the center with wire or string. If a project requires a pompon size that falls between the pre-made sizes (say, 1¾″) buy the next largest pompon and trim it to size.

YARN AND POMPON MAKERS

For hand-made pompons, we use worsted weight yarn. Although other weights can be used, the effect will be different. For the smaller pompons, you may wish to use scrap yarn. If you purchase new yarn, worsted weight usually comes in skeins of 3 oz, 3½ oz or 4 oz. Figure that most yarns yield 60 yds to the ounce in deciding how much to buy.

Hand-made pompons can be made either with a purchased pompon maker, or by making your own cardboard or plastic rings. Purchased pompon makers usually consist of sets of interlocking rings that snap together to make a variety of different sizes of pompons. Instructions are given on the package in most cases. You may, however, still wish to read through the following instructions for making pompons, as the special hints can be used with the purchased pompon makers as well.

To make your own rings, you need to draw a circle with a center hole, then trace this onto cardboard or the plastic lids of coffee cans or margarine tubs. You will need two identical rings for each size pompon. *Fig 1* shows one of the rings for a 1½″ pompon.

The chart below is a guide for cutting the rings for specific diameter pompons, and also specifies the approximate yarn yardage needed for each size.

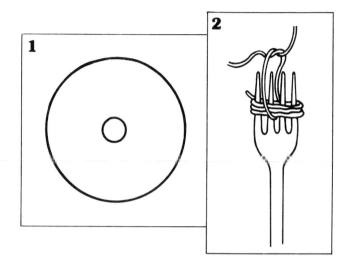

Our yarn amounts are approximate. We prefer a firm, but not tight pompon. You may discover however, that your pompons take additional yarn.

Hint: For very small pompons, wrap the yarn around the tines of a dinner fork; you can use all four, or three, or two tines, depending on the desired pompon diameter. For these small pompons, you may find tying them with doubled thread is better than yarn. *Fig 2* shows the use of the fork.

MAKING A PERFECT POMPON

The following steps should produce a perfect pompon. You may wish to practice with some scrap yarn first to check your tension. A tightly wound pompon will be full and solid, while a loosely wound pompon will be soft and fluffy.

Hint: For ease in winding, thread the yarn into a Size 16 or 14 steel tapestry needle, or into a plastic yarn needle with a large eye. Instructions that come with purchased pompon makers usually don't tell you this, but it's important!

POMPON MAKING GUIDE							
POMPON DIAMETER	1½″	2″	2½″	3″	3½″	4″	4½″
OUTER RING DIAMETER	1½″	1½″	2¼″	2¼″	3″	3¾″	4″
CENTER HOLE DIAMETER	¼″	⅝″	⅝″	1¼″	1¼″	1½″	1¾″
YARN YARDAGE	5–10 yds	8–13 yds	12–17 yds	26–31 yds	35–40 yds	54–59 yds	75–80 yds

Step 1: Cut a piece of yarn at least 5 yds long. Fold yarn in half, and thread the folded end through a needle (*Fig 3*), pulling the folded end through until you have four strands of equal length (*Fig 4*).

Hint: It takes quite a bit of yarn to make a good pompon, and by using four yarn lengths at once you won't have to thread your needle so often.

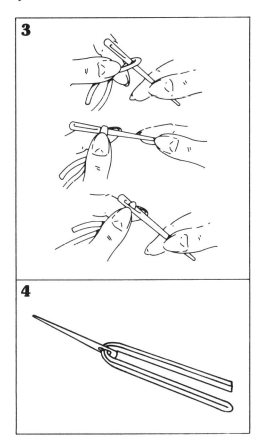

Step 2: Select two of the correct size rings, and hold them together. Draw the needle through the center hole of both rings, and hold the yarn ends against the rings with your index finger (*Fig 5*). Wrap the yarn over the outside edge of the rings, then through the center again; repeat this a few times to secure yarn ends (*Fig 6*). Continue winding around the ring, laying the yarn closely and evenly, until the center hole is filled up. Whenever you run out of yarn, cut off the needle, then thread it again as before. Hold both the new and old ends of yarn together, and wind over both sets of ends to secure.

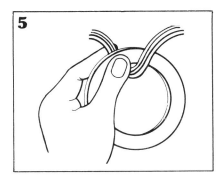

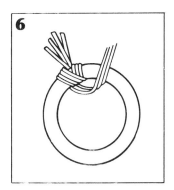

Step 3: When the center hole is filled, cut off the needle and any excess yarn. With *very sharp pointed scissors*, cut the yarn between the two rings (*Fig 7*). Slip your scissors carefully between the two rings, and cut several strands at a time.

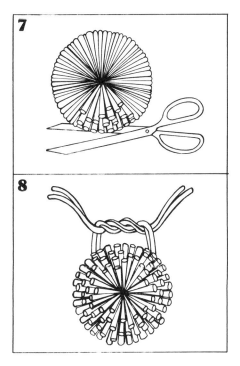

Step 4: Cut two 12″ strands of yarn. To tie the center of the pompon together, slip the two yarn strands between the circles (you may have to gently ease the circles apart a bit), overlap ends two or three times (*Fig 8*), and pull up *very tightly*. Tie yarn ends into a secure knot. Do not cut off ends yet.

Step 5: Remove both rings, wiggling them gently to help them slide off the yarn. Hold the tie ends and shake the pompon to fluff it, then roll it between your hands to mold it into shape. Use the tie ends as a "handle" for working with the pompon.

Step 6: With very sharp scissors, trim the pompon evenly. If pompon is larger than desired, trim off as much as is needed. If you plan to use the ties to attach the pompon to another, or to attach an ornament, do not trim them off. Otherwise, trim ties now to match rest of pompon.

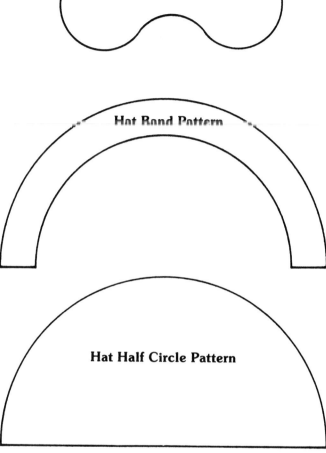

Feet Pattern

Hat Band Pattern

Hat Half Circle Pattern

POMPON SANTA

designed by Carol Wilson Mansfield

This darling Santa would make a perfect package decoration, a Christmas party favor, or (add a string for hanging) a charming tree ornament.

Size

3″ high

Materials

One 3″ white pompon
One ½″ bright pink pompon
One ¼″ white pompon for hat tassel
Black felt (*approx 3″ × 5″*) for feet
Red felt (*approx 3″ × 4″*) for hat
White felt (*approx 2″ × 4″*) for hat band
Iron-on interfacing (*approx 5″ × 5″*)
Two 8mm moving eyes
Tacky craft glue

Instructions

We have given you full-size patterns for felt pieces. First trace the pattern onto the non-fusible side of medium weight iron-on interfacing.

Cut out the interfacing shapes outside the lines, leaving about ¼″ all around the edges. Iron these cut out shapes onto the desired color of felt. Cut out felt shapes on the lines. The result is a felt piece the exact size of the pattern, with interfacing on one side to give it stability.

The feet are to be glued onto a second layer of felt. Follow the above instructions for ironing on and cutting

out one felt shape. Glue that shape, interfacing side down, onto a second piece of felt and trim to match the first.

Step 1: Glue pink pompon nose onto large white pompon.

Step 2: Trace feet and hat patterns.

Step 3: Transfer feet pattern onto black felt and cut out. Glue onto second layer of black and trim. Glue feet securely to base.

Step 4: Transfer half circle hat pattern onto red felt; hat band onto white felt. Cut out both pieces. Fold half circle into a cone shape overlapping bottom edge ¼″. Glue hat band onto bottom edge of hat overlapping edges. Fold over tip of cone to side and glue point down. Glue ¼″ white pompon onto point. Glue hat to top of Santa. Glue on moving eyes.

POMPON
CHRISTMAS TREE

designed by Anita Simes

This shimmering pompon tree will add a truly festive touch to your holiday decorations. Draped with beads and sequins it would make a beautiful table centerpiece, or just picture it on a coffee table surrounded by tiny wrapped boxes. It's really so easy to make. Pins are used to attach the pompons and decorations to a plastic foam base. With a minimum of effort you can create a lasting Christmas decoration that will delight family and friends for many years.

Size
8½" high

Materials
Medium green pompons:
    sixteen 3"
    seven 2½"
    seven 2"
    seven 1½"
    thirteen 1"
Dark green pompons:
    eleven 2"
    ten 1½"

    twenty-five 1"
    seven ½"
Twenty-five ¼" red pompons
One 1½" yellow pompon
One 12" tall plastic foam cone (*use green if available*)
Three packages of 2" craft pins (*approx 165 pins*)
8mm faceted crystal beads (*approx 300 pieces*)
18mm pleated discs in silver and gold (*approx 55 pieces*)
11mm multi-colored tri-beads (*approx 55 pieces*)
Gold leaves 15mm long (*approx 20 pieces*)
Two 12" red chenille stems for candy canes
Two 12" white chenille stems for candy canes
White thread

Instructions

Starting at the bottom of the cone and working up to the top there will be 12 rows of pompons pinned onto the plastic foam base. Each row should be completed before continuing to the next row. The 2" craft pins are stuck through the middle of the pompons and inserted into the cone. The pompons should cover and hide the plastic foam underneath. It may be necessary to adjust the placement of a few pompons as you go along to fill in all the areas. To serve as a guide as you work, the first four rows of pompons should cover the bottom 6" of the cone; the first seven rows should cover 9". As you approach the top of the cone, insert the pins on a downward angle so that they do not pass through the cone and stick out the other side.

Row 1: Beginning at the bottom of the cone, pin eight 3" medium green pompons around the base. Pin eight 1" dark green pompons in between the 3" pompons (see *Fig 1*).

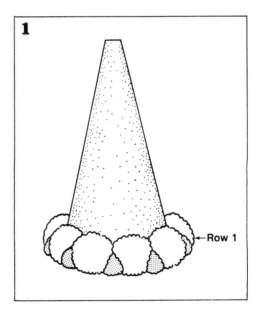

Row 2: Pin eight 3" medium green pompons around cone. For all the remaining rows pin the following pompons around the cone adjusting the spacing when necessary.

Row 3: Eleven 2" dark green

31

Row 4: Seven 2½″ medium green

Row 5: Ten 1½″ dark green

Row 6: Seven 2″ medium green

Row 7: Ten 1″ dark green

Row 8: Seven 1½″ medium green

Row 9: Seven 1″ dark green

Row 10: Seven 1″ medium green

Row 11: Six 1″ medium green

Row 12: Seven ½″ dark green

There are five garlands on the tree.

GARLAND 1: Using the faceted crystal beads and a double thickness of thread (32″ long) string 92 beads onto thread. Tie the ends of the thread together so that beads are loosely strung. (If strung too tightly, the beads will not drape on the tree). Stick a craft pin through a ¼″ red pompon and then through a crystal bead next to the knotted thread (**Fig 2**). Insert the pin into the cone anywhere on row 2. The red pompon will hide the ends of the thread. Using four more pins (without red pompons) drape the garland by sticking each pin through a strung bead and inserting it into cone around row 2 as in the picture.

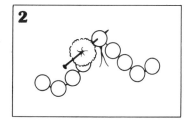

Repeat the above instructions for the next four garlands with the following specifications:

GARLAND 2: Doubled thread 30″ long, 77 crystal beads, one red pompon, 5 craft pins, apply on row 4.

GARLAND 3: Doubled thread 20″ long, 52 crystal beads, one red pompon, 3 craft pins, apply on row 6.

GARLAND 4: Doubled thread 17″ long, 45 crystal beads, one red pompon, 3 craft pins, apply on row 8.

GARLAND 5: Doubled thread 14″ long, 34 crystal beads, one red pompon, 3 craft pins, apply on row 10.

Stick craft pins through red pompons and scatter around tree.

Pin together tri-beads, gold leaves, and pleated discs (**Fig 3**) and scatter on tree.

Stick pins through tri-beads then pleated discs (**Fig 4**) and scatter around tree.

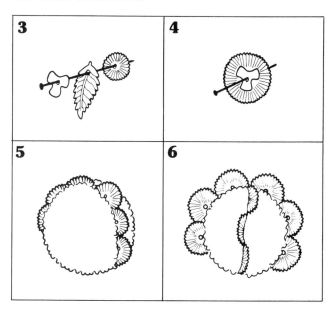

For candy canes, cut chenille stems into 2″ lengths. Twist a red and a white 2″ piece together, curve end to form a cane shape. Hang the canes on the bead garlands.

For tree top ornament, open yellow pompon, apply glue, and insert a row of six gold pleated discs (**Fig 5**). Pinch pompon together around discs until glue sets. Open pompon on either side (perpendicular to first row), apply glue and insert six more gold discs (**Fig 6**). Pinch the pompon to hold the discs and set aside to dry. Secure ornament to top of tree with four pins. Pinch the pompon to hold the discs until the glue sets. Apply glue to the flat side of four more discs and press them onto the pompon between the rows of inserted discs.

PLASTIC CANVAS NEEDLEPOINT

Christmas items have long been favorites of needleworkers, and now you can add a new dimension to your projects with plastic canvas!

Plastic canvas is ideal for gifts, as it works up quickly, and there's no cost of blocking and finishing. The projects in this chapter were designed for gifting, for bazaars, or for decorating your own home.

Even if you've never done needlepoint before, you'll find stitching on plastic canvas is easy, fast and fun.

Plastic canvas has many plusses: it doesn't get out of shape as you stitch, so requires no blocking; the finishing (making up the completed project) is easy enough that you can do it yourself; because the cut edges don't fray, interesting and unusual shapes can be cut; and the projects can be washed (by hand).

PLASTIC CANVAS HOW-TO

THE CANVAS GRID

These projects are all worked on plastic canvas with 7 holes to the inch (often called 7-mesh canvas). We have used three forms of the canvas: rectangular sheets; oval forms for placemats; and circles.

The *rectangular sheets* are available in sizes 10″ × 13½″ (the most commonly used size); and in 12″ × 18″ sheets. When we refer to "sheets" in our instructions, we mean the smaller size unless otherwise specified. Because the canvas does not always have exactly matching holes on both the vertical and horizontal rows, it is important to cut the canvas so that the tops of all the pieces are running the same way. This ensures an exact fit when joining.

The *oval forms* are 12″ by 17½″, and were designed especially for placemats.

Circles are available in 3″ and 4¼″ diameter.

THE PATTERN CHARTS

There is a pattern chart for each piece of each project, which shows where you stitch and with what color. A symbol is used to represent each different color, and a key to these symbols is given with the yarn requirements for each project. Symbols are placed on the charts at the intersection of canvas bars where you will make the given stitch.

THE EQUIPMENT

For stitching, you will need a size 16 steel tapestry needle. For cutting, you will need two pairs of very sharp scissors: a pair of dressmaker-type shears with straight blades for cutting large pieces, and a pair of 7″ embroidery-type scissors with straight blades and sharp points for cutting small areas and trimming off nubs. You also should have a sharp craft knife (we use an X-acto No. 1), or a single edge razor blade; and a china marking pencil (sometimes called a grease pencil) in black or dark blue, which is usually available in stationery departments or office supply stores.

CUTTING THE CANVAS

Cutting the canvas must be done very carefully; if you miscut, the piece is ruined and you'll have to cut another piece.

Cut all the pieces for a project at one time, before you start stitching, being sure that all the pieces are laid out correctly on the canvas, with all the tops in one direction.

Our charts show the shape of the pieces when they are cut out, making it easier for you to follow the cutting line. **To cut, count bars, not holes.** On each chart we give the total maximum number of bars required for each

piece. You may wish to cut the piece into a square or rectangle of the maximum width and length, then stitch the piece; after stitching, do the final cutting. This method is especially good when the piece has a number of stairstep or irregular edges, as it is easy to make a mistake when cutting these before stitching.

Cutting will be easier if you use a china marking pencil (see paragraph on equipment) to draw the cutting outline on the canvas. This pencil will wipe off easily after cutting. For long, straight edges, a ruler helps you draw more quickly.

Cut in the space between bars (**Fig 1**), rather than on a bar. After cutting, you will need to trim off all of the plastic nubs that remain, using the smaller sharp scissors, or, in small hard to reach areas, the craft knife.

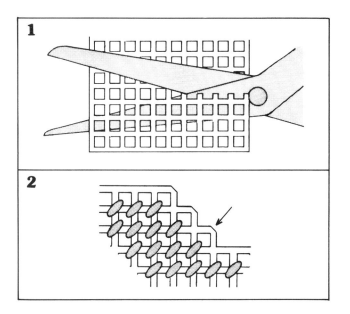

Trimming these nubs cleanly will make your work look much more finished. To make joining and overcasting of open edges neater, cut all corners carefully at a diagonal (**Fig 2**), being careful not to cut so closely that the canvas bar is weakened.

THE YARN

Any yarn that covers the canvas adequately can be used with plastic canvas. For the 7-mesh used in this booklet, for all half cross or continental stitches, we worked with 1 strand of rug, craft or worsted weight yarn. For upright stitches or decorative stitches, additional strands may be required; if so, this is specified in the instructions.

If you prefer to use needlepoint tapestry wool, 2 strands will be needed for the diagonal stitches; and of Persian type wool, use 3 strands. If you are using wool yarns, remember that the project's washability will be affected.

When working with synthetic yarns, cut yarn into 36″ lengths for stitching. For wool yarns, use 18″ lengths to keep yarn from fraying.

THREADING THE NEEDLE

This may take practice, but will become an easy way to thread your tapestry needle. Fold yarn over needle (**Fig 3**). Pinch yarn fold tightly with thumb and first finger (**Fig 4**). Carefully slide needle out of fold and push pinched yarn into needle eye. (**Fig 5**).

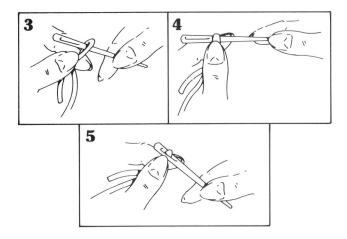

BEGINNING AND ENDING YARN

When beginning to stitch with a new strand of yarn, do not knot yarn. Bring needle up from underside, leaving an inch of yarn on back. Hold end in place with finger while making first few stitches. If adjacent area is already stitched, you may instead run yarn through backs of previous stitches to secure. Backs of stitches will secure end (**Fig 6**). When yarn is too short or a color area is complete, turn canvas over and run needle through backs of a few existing stitches.

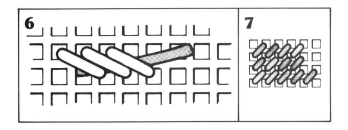

THE STITCHES

Unless otherwise noted in special instructions for each project, the design area is worked in the tent stitch. This forms a flat, diagonal stitch on the front of the canvas (**Fig 7**). The tent stitch can be worked in one of two ways, each of which has an advantage.

METHOD A—CONTINENTAL STITCH: To work horizontal rows, bring needle up through canvas at odd numbers, down at even, as shown in **Fig 8**. First row is worked from right to left, next row from left to right. This method is slightly different than used in regular needlepoint, because our method is easier to understand and does not require turning the canvas upside down for alternate rows (this can make following a chart confusing).

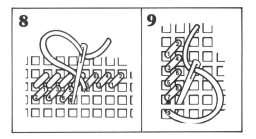

To work vertical rows (used only when there is a long area of just one stitch in width), work as in **Fig 9**.

Advantage: Continental Stitch gives a padded back, which is desirable for items such as placemats. It also makes the stitching appear a little fuller, giving better coverage.

METHOD B—HALF CROSS STITCH: To work horizontal rows, bring needle up at odd numbers, down at even, as in **Figure 10**. First row is worked from left to right, second row from right to left. Again we have adapted the stitch so that work does not have to be turned upside down at the end of each row.

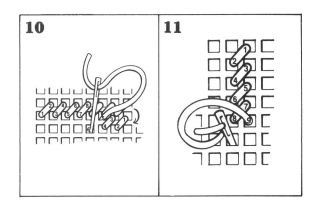

To work vertical rows, work as in **Fig 11**.

Advantage: Half Cross Stitch uses two-thirds as much yarn as does Continental to cover the same area. If you are making a large number of items, such as for a bazaar, this could be a significant cost-saving factor.

DECORATIVE STITCHES: Some of the designs use decorative stitches that are fun to stitch and give interesting texture to the projects. When a decorative stitch is used, we give complete instructions for working it in the individual instructions for each project.

COMPENSATING STITCHES: Often when a decorative stitch is used, there will be places at the top, sides or bottom, or when working around a design, where a unit of the decorative stitch cannot be worked completely. You must adjust, or *compensate* for this by working the stitch unit with some shorter or longer stitches. This is called *working compensating stitches.*

JOINING AND FINISHING

For finishing open edges, or for joining pieces of the projects, we use the Overcast Stitch.

OVERCAST STITCH: This stitch can be worked either from right to left, or left to right, whichever is more comfortable for you. All edges that are not to be joined must be Overcast (or worked in the Binding Stitch).

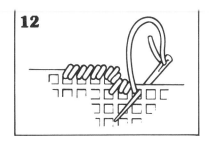

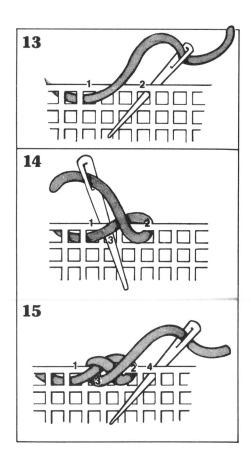

Work stitch as in **Fig 12**, taking 2 stitches in each hole along sides, and 3 stitches in each corner hole.

To join with Overcasting, hold two pieces with wrong sides together and holes carefully aligned. Work Overcast Stitch as before, going through both pieces each time.

You may use a knot to anchor thread (carefully hidden on the back, of course) when beginning to Overcast. When ending off, secure yarn by weaving through the backs of several stitches. It is important to join and end off securely when joining pieces, as often pressure is put on these joinings in the construction.

BINDING STITCH: This stitch is more difficult to learn than Overcasting, but the beautiful, braided effect is well worth the effort. It can be worked easily along a straight edge and around a corner, but is not suitable for shaped, uneven edges.

The stitch is always worked from left to right, with the right side of the stitched canvas facing you. Work as follows:

Step 1: Secure yarn in previous stitching, then bring needle up at 1, down around edge bar and up at 2 (**Fig 13**).

Step 2: Bring needle back to the left two holes, over and around edge bar, and up at 3 (**Fig 14**), one hole to the right of where yarn first came up in previous stitch.

Step 3: Bring needle to the right three holes, over and around edge bar, and up at 4 (**Fig 15**), one hole to the right of where yarn came up before.

Repeat Steps 2 and 3 for stitch; note attractive braid that forms on top edge. It will be easy to remember this stitch if you remember "back 2 holes (Step 2), forward 1 hole (Step 3)."

To turn corners, work to corner, then take two or three extra overcast stitches in corner. Work across next side, first working Step 1 again, using the corner hole for bringing needle up at 1.

When joining two pieces with the Binding Stitch, be sure to line holes up carefully, and work through both pieces of canvas at the same time.

TACKING STITCH: Tacking stitches are used to join two pieces invisibly. To tack, use a yarn of the same color as the top piece. Fasten yarn securely, then come up and go down as in **Fig 16**, working over an existing stitch. Move over a few stitches and repeat; take as many tacking stitches as you feel are needed. Fasten yarn off securely on wrong side.

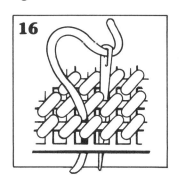

CHRISTMAS PLACEMAT, COASTER AND NAPKIN RING

designed by Carol Wilson Mansfield

Colorful Christmas ribbons intertwine to make this striking holiday set. Our materials will make one complete set.

Size

Placemat, 12" × 17½"
Coaster, 3⅛" square,
Napkin ring, 2" wide

Materials

1 oval placemat form, 12" × 17½"
7-mesh plastic canvas: 7" × 7" piece
Cork backing: 3" × 3" (*for one coaster*)
Worsted weight yarn:

COLOR	YARDS
cream	67
bright blue	9
lt green	27
dk green	44
red	27
dk red	14

PLACEMAT

Instructions

STITCHING PLAN: Once the framework of the main ribbons is established, the piece is quite easy to stitch. Carefully counting out from center, first work the outer rows of lt green on the two center ribbons (both horizontal and vertical). Next work outer rows of remaining ribbons. Then fill in ribbon centers as desired. Last work cream background. Overcast edges with cream. Take care not to stitch too tightly.

COASTER AND NAPKIN RING

Instructions

STITCHING PLAN: Cut out pieces, then stitch following chart. On coaster, overcast edges with cream. Cut cork slightly smaller than outer edge of coaster, glue on, let sit with a weight overnight.

For napkin ring, after stitching, with wrong sides together, overcast short edges to join, using yarn to match adjacent stitches. Overcast both remaining edges with cream.

PLACEMAT

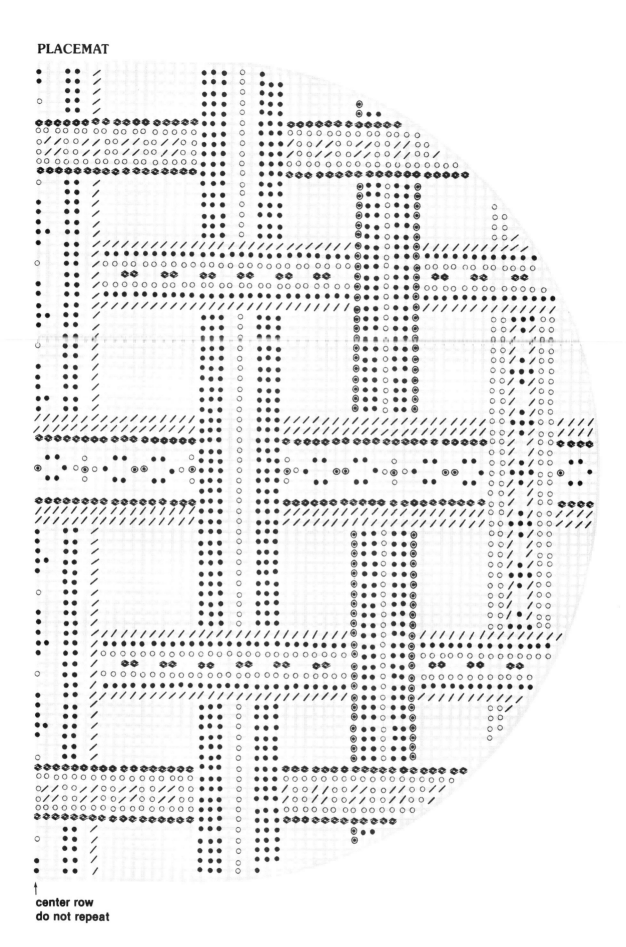

↑
**center row
do not repeat**

38

COASTER

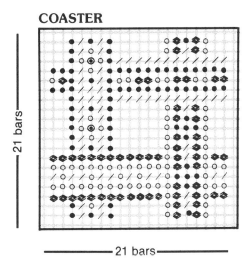

21 bars

21 bars

NAPKIN RING

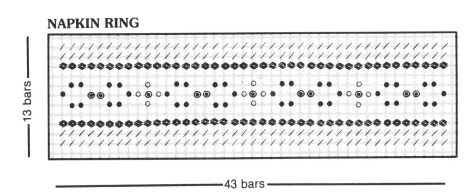

13 bars

43 bars

COLOR KEY

⬜ = Cream

◉ = Bright blue

∕ = Lt green

● = Dk green

○ = Red

◈ = Dk red

each half circle (**Fig 1**). With brown, overcast across sides and front edges to Top Unit (back edge is left free for joining to Bottom Unit later).

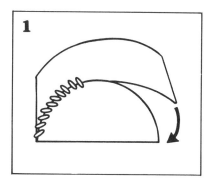

STITCHING PLAN (bottom unit): Cut Front, Back, 2 Side pieces, and Bottom. Cut out two handles. Stitch Side pieces, first working floral bands, then background in brown. Overcast handles as shown in **Fig 2** with brown, then join to Side pieces as shown in **Fig 3**. Stitch Front and Back pieces in same manner, following charts. With brown, overcast Front, Back and Sides to join (**Fig 3**). Overcast unstitched bottom piece to unit with brown. With brown, overcast top edge of Sides and front of Bottom Unit.

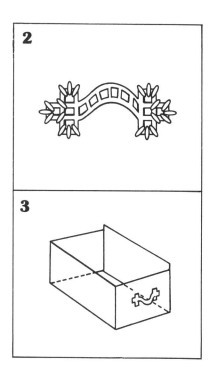

LITTLE TRUNK GIFT BOX

designed by Solveig Carlson

This charming little box can hold a very special gift, candy, playing cards, or whatever. Though festive for the holidays, its colors let it be used as a year-round accessory.

Size

4¼″ × 3¼″ × 3½″ high

Materials

1 sheet 7-mesh plastic canvas
1 set brass closure hardware, about 1¼″ long
3″ plastic canvas circles: 2
Brown felt, piece 3″ × 4″
Worsted weight yarn:

COLOR	YARDS
brown	25
red	6
lt green	6
dk green	6
white	3

Instructions

STITCHING PLAN (top unit): Cut out top rectangle and stitch following chart. First stitch floral bands, then fill in background. For rounded end pieces, cut two 3″ diameter circles and stitch as on chart. With brown, overcast and join one long side of Top rectangle to curved edge of

Construction and Finishing

Place Top Unit on top of Bottom Unit and overcast back edges together. Sew brass hardware on front. Cut brown felt to fit bottom, place inside. You may line entire inside with felt if desired (additional felt will be required). If lining stitched areas, glue felt in place.

TOP

31 bars

28 bars

SIDE (make 2)

12 bars

21 bars

FRONT

12 bars

28 bars

BACK

13 bars

28 bars

HANDLE (make 2)

4 bars

11 bars

BOTTOM (cut piece 28 bars × 21 bars)

unstitched

TOP SIDE (make 2)

^ ^ ^   stitch these 3 rows lt green
all others brown

COLOR KEY

  = Brown   ◎ = Dk green

● = Red   ○ = White

+ = Lt green

41

THE LITTLE LOG CABIN IN THE WOODS

designed by Don FranzMeier

Santa's sled is parked on the roof of the little log cabin, and lighted windows offer a welcome on this cold night. Make the cabin as a special Christmas display item; use it as a centerpiece; place it on your mantle, or under the Christmas tree.

For ease in construction, roofs and other details are glued on. Because it gives a flexible bond, we used general purpose silicone sealant (available in a tube at hardware stores). This sealant sets in a few minutes and dries completely in 24 hours. Wait at least five minutes between gluing each section to allow for setting. The sealant dries clearly and when dry, excess can be trimmed with a craft knife. Tacky glue can be used, if you prefer.

You'll enjoy decorating the Little Log Cabin, using small plastic figures, trees, and polyester stuffing for the snow. The plastic figures, bushes and trees are available at craft stores. For the taller trees, try model train departments. Attach the decorations with the silicone sealant or tacky glue.

Size

Approximately 10″ × 8″ × 8″

Materials

3 sheets 7-mesh plastic canvas
Worsted weight yarn:

COLOR	YARDS
yellow	8
red	2
rust	10
brown	70
grey	22
black	2
white	45

Silicone sealant or tacky craft glue

Instructions

STITCHING PLAN: Cut out all pieces and stitch following charts. Stitch windows and doors first on wall pieces, then fill in background. Backstitch around windows with brown as indicated on charts. The side of the Right Wing Unit that abuts the Left Wing Unit is unstitched. Cut bottom piece for left wing unit 23 bars × 29 bars and leave unstitched. Cut bottom piece for right wing unit 15 bars × 27 bars and leave unstitched.

Assembly

LEFT WING UNIT: Join wall pieces 1, 2, 3 and 4 with brown, then overcast all top edges. Join bottom edges to unstitched bottom piece with grey. For roof, join pieces 5 and 6 at long edge and overcast edges with brown. Glue roof to top edge of wall unit.

RIGHT WING UNIT: Join pieces 7, 8, 9 and 10 (this piece is not stitched), with brown and overcast top edges of unit. Join bottom edge to unstitched bottom piece with grey. For roof, join pieces 11 and 12 at long edge, then overcast edges with brown.

CHIMNEY: With rust, join pieces 16, 17 and 18 along short edges as shown in construction diagram. Join this strip to piece 13 along shaped edge. Join piece 14 to remaining long straight edge of piece 13. Join piece 15 to edges of pieces 14 and 16, keeping even at top. Glue chimney unit to piece 7 as shown.

FENCE AND YARD: Carefully cut out all 14 pieces (F) and trim nubs. With brown, overcast around inside edges of 19, 20, 21 and all (F) pieces and join at short edges with top edges even. Overcast top edge of entire fence with brown. Overcast bottom edge of (F) pieces only with brown. Note: (F) pieces are one bar shorter than rest of fence. Join fence pieces 19, 20 and 21 to yard (22) with white. With white, tack (F) fence pieces to yard at seams.

Finishing

Glue unstitched side of Right Wing Unit to Left Wing Unit. Glue log cabin in position on yard. Add miniature figures, trees and decorations as desired.

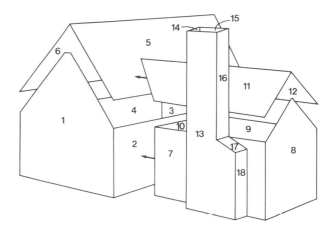

COLOR KEY

o	=	Yellow tent stitch	/	= White pattern stitch
♠	=	Grey tent stitch	⟋	= Rust pattern stitch
◉	=	Red tent stitch	/	= Brown pattern stitch
★	=	Brown tent stitch	.....	= Brown back stitch
■	=	Black tent stitch	•	= Black French knot

LEFT WING UNIT

①③
FRONT/BACK (make 2)

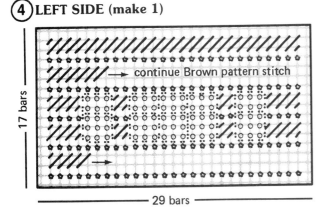

— 23 bars —
27 bars

continue Brown pattern stitch

⑤⑥
ROOF (make 2)

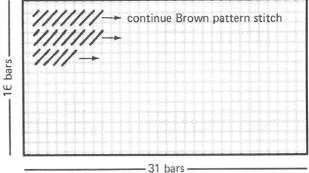

continue Brown pattern stitch

16 bars
— 31 bars —

④ LEFT SIDE (make 1)

17 bars
continue Brown pattern stitch
— 29 bars —

② RIGHT SIDE (make 1)

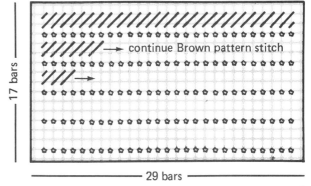

17 bars
continue Brown pattern stitch
— 29 bars —

(Pattern charts continue on next page)

43

⑦ **FRONT (make 1)**

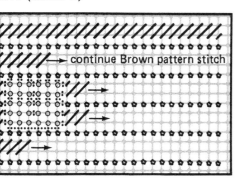

17 bars

27 bars

RIGHT WING UNIT

⑧ **RIGHT SIDE (make 1)**

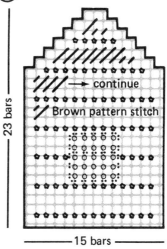

23 bars

15 bars

⑩ **LEFT SIDE (make 1)**

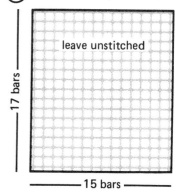

17 bars

leave unstitched

15 bars

⑨ **BACK (make 1)**

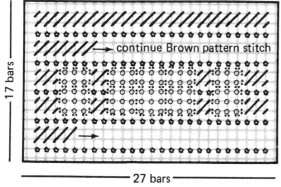

17 bars

27 bars

COLOR KEY

o	= Yellow tent stitch		/	= White pattern stitch
⬠	= Grey tent stitch		⫶	= Rust pattern stitch
◉	= Red tent stitch		/	= Brown pattern stitch
★	= Brown tent stitch		·····	= Brown back stitch
■	= Black tent stitch		•	= Black French knot

CHIMNEY

⑮ **UPPER BACK (make 1)**

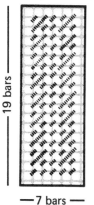

19 bars

7 bars

⑭ **LEFT SIDE (make 1)**

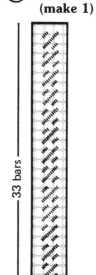

33 bars

4 bars

⑬ **FRONT (make 1)**

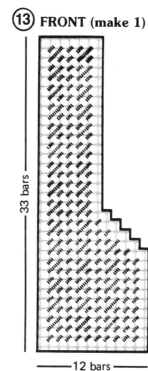

33 bars

12 bars

⑯ **UPPER RIGHT SIDE (make 1)**

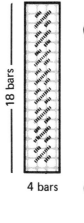

18 bars

4 bars

⑰ **LEDGE RIGHT SIDE (make 1)**

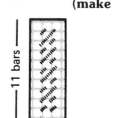

8 bars

4 bars

⑱ **LOWER RIGHT SIDE (make 1)**

11 bars

4 bars

ROOF

⑪ ROOF FRONT (make 1)

continue Brown pattern stitch

— 35 bars —

⑫ ROOF BACK (make 1)

continue Brown pattern stitch

11 bars

— 35 bars —

FENCE & YARD

⑲ ㉑ FENCE SIDE (make 2)

6 bars

— 33 bars —

Ⓕ FENCE FRONT (make 14)

5 bars

— 8 bars —

⑳ FENCE BACK (make 1)

6 bars

— 71 bars —

㉒ YARD (make 1)

continue White pattern stitch

continue White pattern stitch

47 bars

— 71 bars —

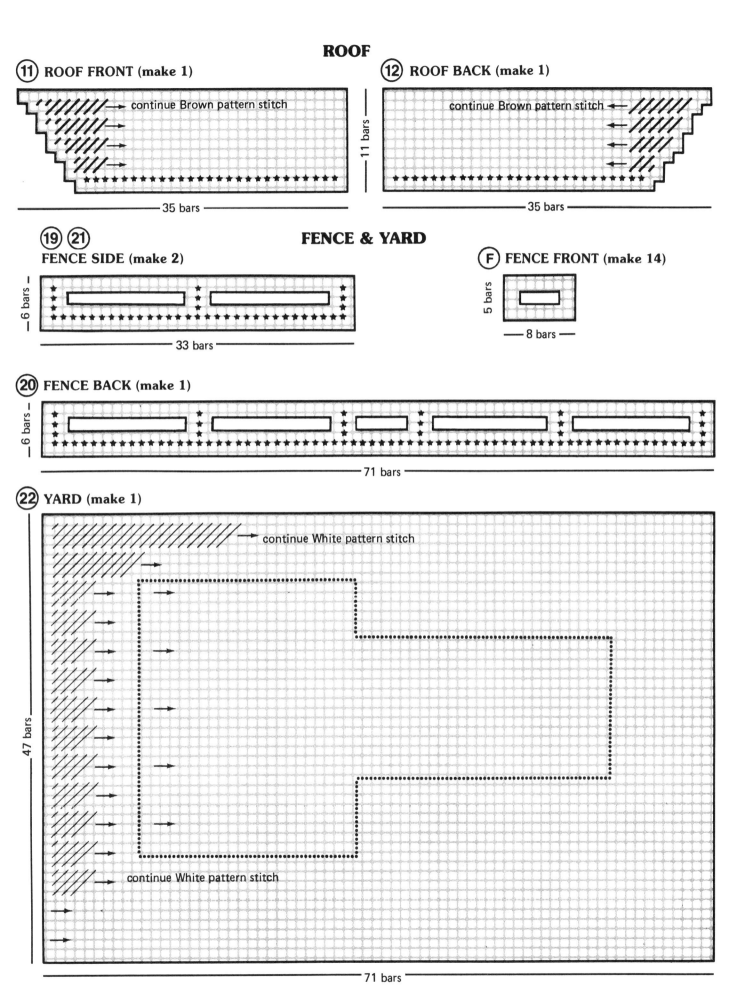

45

CHRISTMAS COTTAGE

designed by Carol Wilson Mansfield

This is surely an enchanted cottage, to fill with cookies, candies, small gifts, or to use as a centerpiece. Because plastic canvas is washable (by hand, of course), crumbs can be taken care of at the end of the season. Although the cottage has several pieces, it is not difficult to stitch or to construct.

Size

6½" long
5" wide
7½" high

Materials

3 sheets 7-mesh plastic canvas
Gold metallic needlepoint thread: 1 yard
2 small gold beads for doorknob or miniature doorknobs
Worsted weight yarn:

COLOR	YARDS
white	65
cream	2
lt blue	4
med blue	6
yellow	1
lt green	14
med green	35
dk green	3

COLOR	YARDS
bright red	12
cranberry	60
lt brown	7
dk brown	10
Gold needlepoint thread	2

46

ROOF

Instructions

First cut out the two rectangular roof side pieces. Next cut the two gable pieces to the maximum rectangular shape. You will stitch the gables *before* cutting out completely.

STITCHING PLAN: On each roof piece, first stitch the red and green motifs. To make sure motifs are placed correctly, first stitch one complete horizontal row across the top, then one complete vertical row along one side. This way you can see if subsequent motifs are placed correctly. Last, fill in white background with Continental stitch. Place two roof pieces with wrong sides together, and overcast with white to join along top long edge. With white, overcast remaining edges.

On gables, first stitch wreath. With red yarn work French knots (*Fig 1*) on top of green stitching where indicated by dots on chart. Fill in background with Diagonal Gobelin stitch (*Fig 2*). *NOTE: 1 strand of worsted weight will usually cover well in this stitch. If you feel the coverage is not good, however, use two strands (additional yarn will be required).*

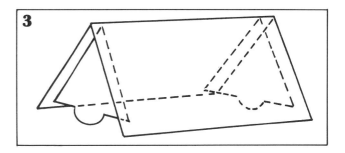

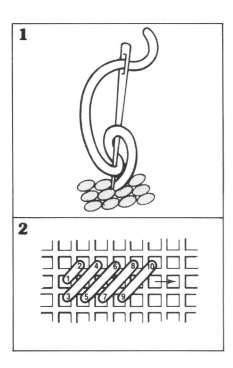

Now cut out gables, carefully trimming stair-step edges to remove nubs. Overcast all three gable outer edges with cranberry yarn. Place one gable in one end of roof along third bar in from edge of roof (*Fig 3*). Starting at peak, tack firmly with white sewing thread along each diagonal edge. Repeat at opposite end. Set completed unit aside.

HOUSE

Instructions

SIDE UNITS: Cut out two Sides, two Upper Sides, and 8 Shutters. Stitch Sides following chart, first working windows. Note that on both sides of each window, one vertical row is left unstitched for later joining of Shutter. Next work shrubbery, then fill in background with cranberry in Diagonal Gobelin stitch.

Stitch all 8 Shutters in white, working Continental stitch in center row of each piece. Overcast top and bottom and one side of each Shutter in white. Place long side of Shutter on top of unworked bar at side of a window and overcast through both layers. Do this on both sides of all four windows.

With cranberry, work both Upper Side pieces in Diagonal Gobelin. Place one long edge of Upper Side piece along top edge of Side, right sides together. With cranberry, overcast to join. Finish other Side unit the same.

BACK OF COTTAGE: Following chart, stitch windows, shrubbery and Shutters as for Sides. Attach Shutters in same manner. Fill in background with Diagonal Gobelin in cranberry.

FRONT OF COTTAGE: Stitch Front following chart, leaving bars around door opening unstitched as shown on chart. Tree decorations are worked in gold metallic thread (you may need two strands of the metallic to cover well). With bright red, work French knots for holly around garland on top and sides of door. Following chart, cut out door frame. From center of frame, cut out door. Carefully

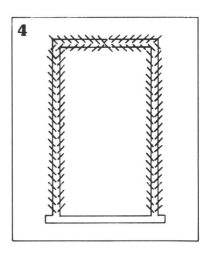

trim all nubs. Stitch door following chart; overcast top, bottom and right side with brown.

Put door frame piece in place. With white, join as shown in *Fig 4*, working through both layers of canvas. Attach top row only of doorstep with light brown. With dark brown, overcast and join left edge of door to remaining unstitched row at left of door opening; use moderate tension so that door will open freely. Sew gold beads on gold stitches on each side of door for handles or glue on miniature doorknobs.

Assembly

Overcasting with cranberry, join Front piece to Side, working from top of Upper Side to beginning of shrubbery; finish off cranberry, complete joining with med green. Join Front to second Side in same manner. Join Back to Side units in same manner (*Fig 5*). Overcast top edges of house with cranberry. Leave bottom piece un-

stitched. Join to bottom edge of all four Sides overcasting with med green up to doorstep. Overcast through 3 layers (doorstep and bottom piece) with light brown. Set roof unit on cottage.

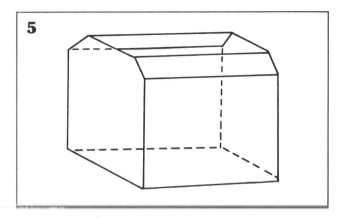

ROOF SIDE (make 2)

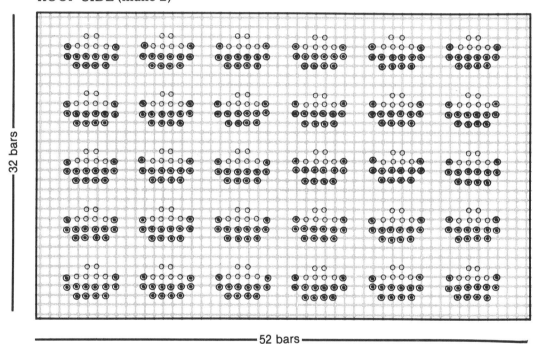

32 bars

52 bars

GABLE (make 2)

22 bars

36 bars

48

BACK

37 bars

34 bars

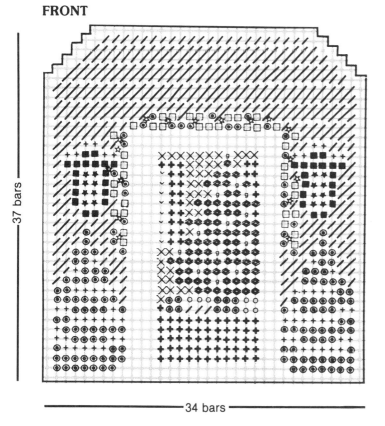

FRONT

37 bars

34 bars

DOOR & DOOR FRAME

26 bars

18 bars

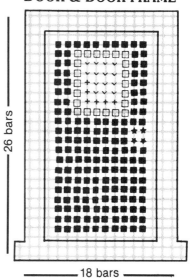

COLOR KEY

⌷ or + = White

× = Cream

˅ = Lt blue

✚ = Med blue

✿ = Yellow

□ = Lt green

◉ = Med green

◈ = Dk green

○ = Bright red

╱ = Cranberry

● = Lt brown

■ = Dk brown

✿ = Bright red French knots

g = Gold needlepoint thread

(Pattern charts continue on next page)

49

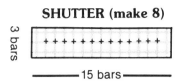

SHUTTER (make 8)

3 bars

————— 15 bars —————

UPPER SIDE (make 2)

8 bars

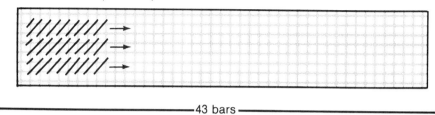

——————————— 43 bars ———————————

SIDE (make 2)

32 bars

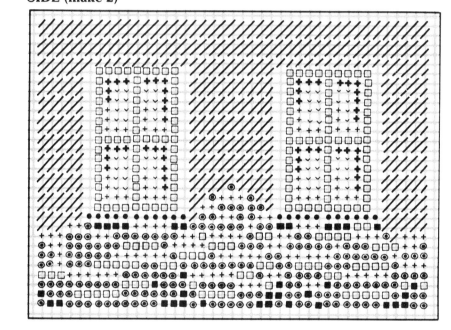

——————————— 43 bars ———————————

COLOR KEY

⬚ or + = White	⬢ =	Dk green
✕ = Cream	○ =	Bright red
⌄ = Lt blue	╱ =	Cranberry
✚ = Med blue	● =	Lt brown
✹ = Yellow	◼ =	Dk brown
☐ = Lt green	✿ =	Bright red French knots
◉ = Med green	ɡ =	Gold needlepoint thread

50

SANTA CENTERPIECE

designed by Anita Simes

This colorful Santa figure can be a centerpiece or mantle decoration. Fill his pack with candy canes or greenery.

Size
9″ tall

Materials
1 sheet 7-mesh plastic canvas
6″ tall plastic foam cone
Candy canes (*optional*)
Worsted Weight yarn:

COLOR	YARDS
white	12
cream	3
pink	1
bright pink	small piece
gold	2
red	12
dk red	2

COLOR	YARDS
bright blue	small piece
green	9
lt brown	3
lt grey	13
charcoal grey	5
black	2

Instructions
STITCHING PLAN: You may find it easier to draw the outline of the two Santa pieces on your sheet of canvas, using a grease pencil and then carefully cut them out before stitching. Following the chart, stitch the Front and Back pieces. Use two strands of yarn in needle when stitching candy cane and beard. Cross stitches are used for the nose and center of belt buckle. Eyebrows are straight stitches worked on top of pink Continental stitches. Work eyes with blue in French knots (*Fig 1*).

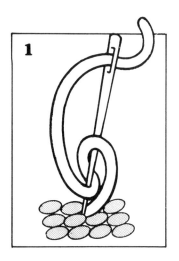

Finishing and Assembly

Overcast bottom edge of Front piece with white, and overcast bottom edge of Back piece matching adjacent stitch colors. With grey, overcast the diagonal edge of sack on both Front and Back pieces. With wrong sides together, overcast Back and Front pieces together, leaving bottom edges and overcast edges of sack open. Overcast with yarn to match adjacent stitches. Place finished piece on top of plastic foam cone for stability. Insert candy canes or greenery in opening of sack.

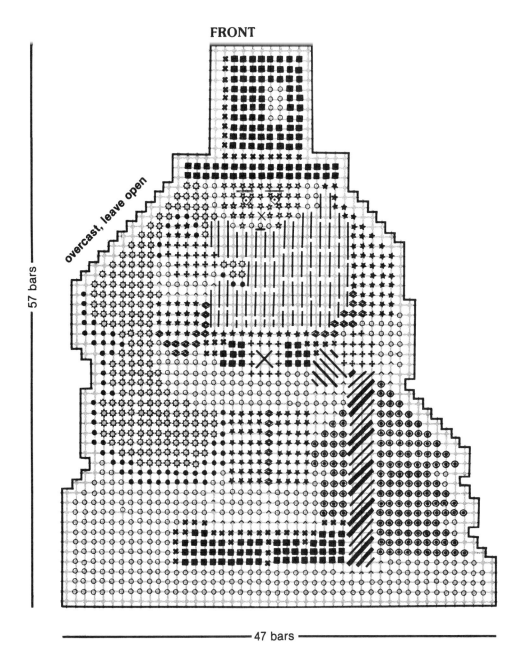

FRONT

overcast, leave open

57 bars

47 bars

COLOR KEY

- o = White
- ^ = Cream
- ✿ = Pink
- ✕ = Bright pink
- + = Gold
- ★ = Red
- ◈ = Dk red
- ◇ = Bright blue
- ◉ = Green
- • = Lt brown
- ✿ = Lt grey
- ■ = Charcoal grey
- ✖ = Black

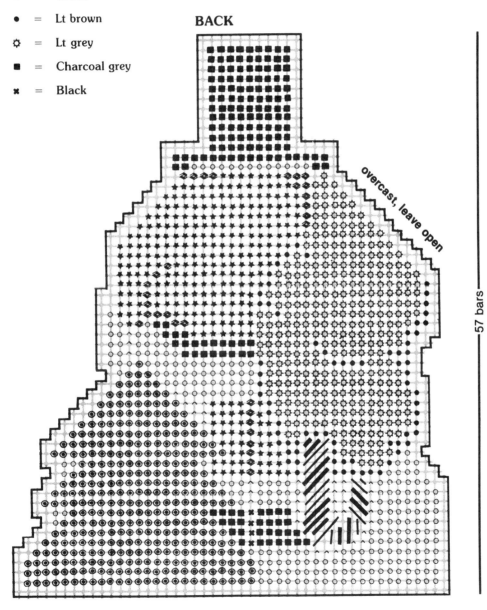

BACK

overcast, leave open

57 bars

47 bars

53

CHRISTMAS PARTY TABLE DECORATIONS

designed by Don FranzMeier

These festive pieces can be used throughout the Christmas season. The beautiful placemat features holly leaves and berries, with an interesting textured stitch for the center. The charming sleigh sits on a snowy ground and is decorated with 3-dimensional holly leaves and shiny red beads for berries. Fill the sleigh with small gift-wrapped packages or tree ornaments. A set of placemats would make a lovely gift or bazaar item.

Size

Placemat, 12″ × 18″
Napkin ring, 1″ wide
Centerpiece, 6″ high

Materials

7-mesh plastic canvas:
    four 11″ × 14″ sheets for sleigh and 4 napkin rings
    one 12″ × 18″ sheet for each placemat
red plastic pony beads:
    33 for sleigh and 4 napkin rings
Tacky craft glue

Worsted weight yarn:	RED	GREEN	BLACK	WHITE
yds for sleigh and 4 napkin rings	45	60	30	110
yds for each placemat	25	25	—	125

PLACEMAT

Instructions

STITCHING PLAN: The chart shows one half of the finished mat; turn chart to work other half.

Step 1: Starting at upper left-hand corner, work red inner border of 2 Continental Stitch rows. Carefully count to place first stitch 18 bars down from top edge, and 18 bars in from left edge. Turn chart and canvas and complete other side of border.

Step 2: Now fill in center area with Giant Diagonal Mosaic Stitch. Work as in *Fig 1*, bringing needle up at 1 and all odd numbers, down at 2 and all even numbers. The stitch is worked diagonally, from upper left to lower

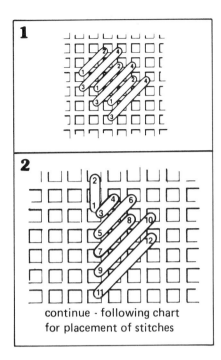

right. Begin at upper left of area (see chart) and work in complete rows diagonally from top to bottom, ending row at red inner border. (*NOTE: Work all rows completely from top to bottom, even if row is completed on the other half of chart.*)

Step 3: With green, next work holly leaf corner motifs as in *Fig 2*, bringing needle up at odd numbers and down at even numbers. Remember to turn chart and canvas to work second half of placemat.

Step 4: With red, work holly berries in Continental Stitch. Be sure to keep all Continental Stitches going in the same direction on all four corners.

Step 5: With red, work Overcast Stitch around all four outer edges.

NAPKIN RING

Instructions

Step 1: Stitch both pieces with white Continental. With red, overcast long edges of each piece. Join with red along short ends.

Step 2: With green, stitch one holly leaf and overcast edges. To give leaf dimension, fold in thirds and fasten tightly with a rubber band (*Fig 3*). Leave band in place for about a half hour. Remove band, and leaf will have a permanent curve.

Step 3: With green, sew holly leaf to top of napkin ring, with bottom edge of leaf centered on top piece. With red, sew 3 red beads on holly leaf at bottom edge.

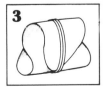

SLEIGH CENTERPIECE

Instructions

Step 1: With white, stitch base in Giant Diagonal Mosaic as for center area of placemat (Step 2 of placemat). Start in upper left-hand corner and work in diagonal rows. Because the wrong side of two corners will be showing, be careful to keep yarn ends from showing on wrong side of corner area. Fold two opposite corners over (about 3¼″ from corner point to fold) as shown in *Fig 4*, and tack points in place with white yarn.

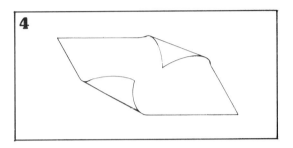

Step 2: With green, make 10 leaves as in Step 2 of napkin ring. Shape with rubber bands in same manner. Set leaves and base aside.

Step 3: For sleigh sides, with red stitch 4 pieces in Horizontal Mosaic Stitch, worked as in *Fig 5*. Bring needle up at 1 and odd numbers, down at 2 and even numbers. Bottom row of each side piece is worked in Continental. Place 2 side pieces with wrong sides together and overcast outer edges with green. Repeat for other 2 side pieces.

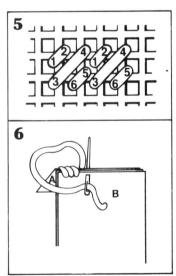

Step 4: With red, stitch all 6 floor pieces in Half Cross Stitch. Hold both B pieces with wrong sides together, and overcast through both pieces **and** through Piece A to join (*Fig 6*); join the other end of the B pieces, working through both pieces, to short edge of Piece C. Hold both D pieces with wrong sides together and overcast through both pieces **and** through remaining short edge of Piece C. Overcast all outer edges with red.

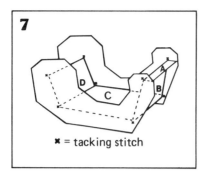

x = tacking stitch

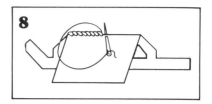

Step 5: With red, tack sleigh floor to side units (*Fig 7*), making sure right side of sleigh floor Piece C is facing up.

Step 6: With black, stitch 4 runner pieces and runner support piece in Continental. With wrong sides together, overcast 2 runner pieces together (including inside edges), leaving top edge unstitched for joining to support piece. Repeat with other 2 runner pieces. With black, overcast short edge of support piece.

Step 7: With black, overcast top edge of each runner unit to long edge of support piece (*Fig 8*).

Step 8: With black, securely tack bottom edge of runners to base, placing as in photo.

Step 9: Glue bottom edge of sleigh side units to outer edges of runner support piece.

Step 10: With red, sew 3 red beads at bottom edge of 7 holly leaves. With green, tack leaves in place as shown in photo.

NOTE: To make the centerpiece easier to handle and store, you may wish to mount it on a cardboard base made from heavy illustration board. Cut the base about ½" less in length and width than the plastic canvas base. Glue together.

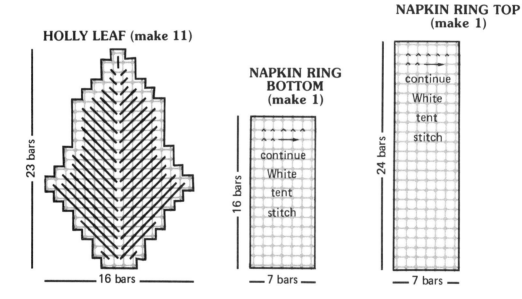

HOLLY LEAF (make 11)

23 bars

16 bars

NAPKIN RING BOTTOM (make 1)

continue White tent stitch

16 bars

7 bars

NAPKIN RING TOP (make 1)

continue White tent stitch

24 bars

7 bars

COLOR KEY

● = Red tent stitch

╱ = White pattern stitch

╱ = Green pattern stitch

╱ = Red pattern stitch

^ = White tent stitch

PLACEMAT ———————— 127 bars ————————

85 bars

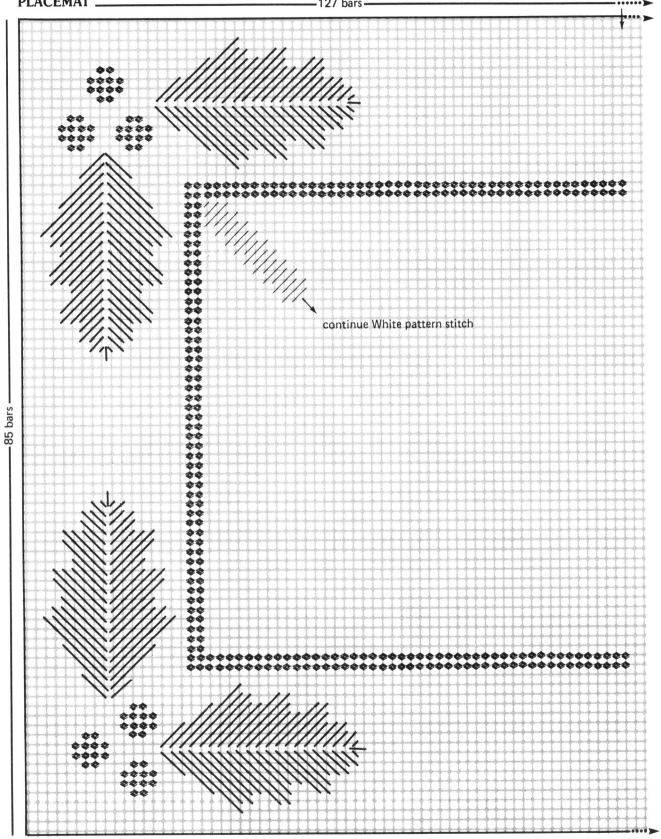

continue White pattern stitch

(Pattern charts continue on next page)

57

SLEIGH SIDE (make 2)

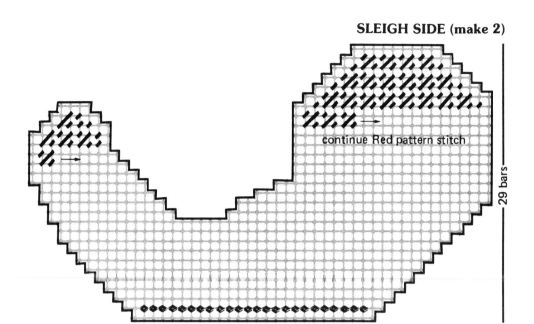

continue Red pattern stitch

29 bars

49 bars

COLOR KEY

⬢	=	Red tent stitch
╱	=	White pattern stitch
╱	=	Green pattern stitch
╱	=	Red pattern stitch

SLEIGH SIDE (make 2)

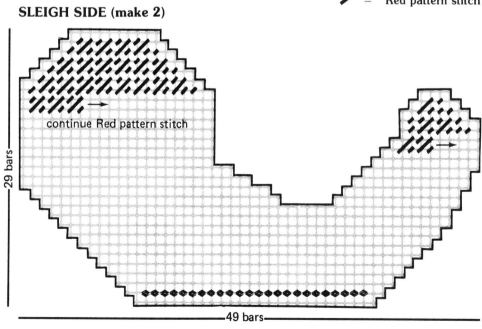

continue Red pattern stitch

29 bars

49 bars

SLEIGH FLOOR A (make 1)

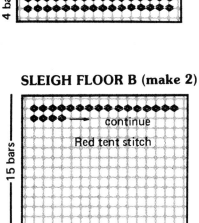

4 bars

SLEIGH FLOOR C (make 1)

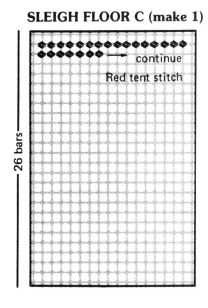

26 bars

continue

Red tent stitch

SLEIGH FLOOR D (make 2)

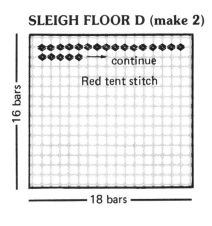

16 bars

continue

Red tent stitch

18 bars

SLEIGH FLOOR B (make 2)

15 bars

continue

Red tent stitch

SLEIGH RUNNER (make 2)

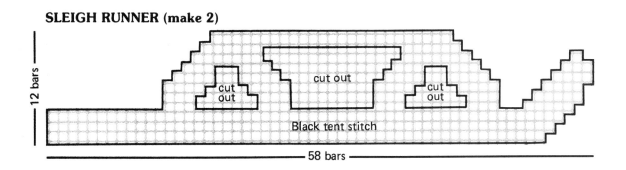

12 bars

cut out

cut out

cut out

Black tent stitch

58 bars

SLEIGH RUNNER (make 2)

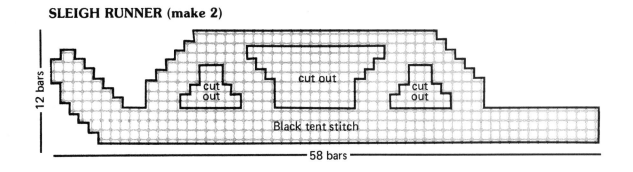

12 bars

cut out

cut out

cut out

Black tent stitch

58 bars

(Pattern charts continue on next page)

SLEIGH RUNNER SUPPORT (make 1)

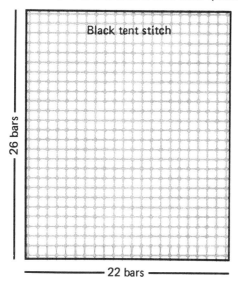

Black tent stitch

26 bars

22 bars

COLOR KEY

●	=	Red tent stitch
╱	=	White pattern stitch
╱	=	Green pattern stitch
╱	=	Red pattern stitch

CENTERPIECE BASE (make 1) — 91 bars —

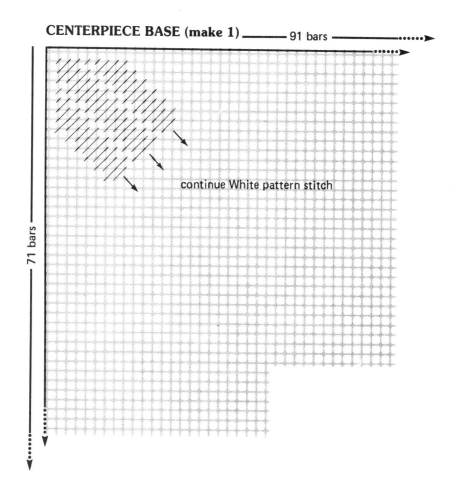

continue White pattern stitch

71 bars

60

CHRISTMAS CHURCH

designed by Don FranzMeier

Our charming church has glowing stained glass windows, and can be used on a mantle or as a centerpiece. We hung a real brass bell (optional) in its belfry.

For ease in construction, roofs and other details are glued on. Because it gives a flexible bond, we used general purpose silicone sealant (available in a tube at hardware stores). This sealant sets in 5 minutes and dries completely in 24 hours. Wait at least 5 minutes between gluing each section to allow for setting. The sealant dries clearly, and when dry, excess can be trimmed with a craft knife. Tacky glue can be used, if you prefer.

You'll enjoy decorating the church, using small plastic figures, trees, and polyester stuffing for the snow. The plastic figures, bushes and trees are available at craft stores. For the taller trees, or for a larger variety, try model train departments or stores. Attach the decorations with the silicone sealant, or tacky glue.

Size

8½″ × 8½″

Materials

2 sheets 7-mesh plastic canvas
Silicone sealant or tacky craft glue
Worsted weight yarn:

COLOR	YARDS
yellow	2
orange	2
red	4
bright blue	2
green	4
purple	2
white	80
grey	50
black	10

Instructions

STITCHING PLAN: Cut out all pieces and stitch following charts. Make yellow French knots for door handles after piece is stitched. On windows, stitch black outline first, then fill in colored area. Cut bottom piece 23 bars × 39 bars and leave unstitched.

Assembly

WALL UNIT: Join pieces 1, 2, 3 and 4 with white. Overcast around top edge of entire unit with white. Join unstitched bottom piece to bottom of unit with white. For door overhang, join pieces 5 and 6, along short edges, then overcast all sides with grey.

ROOF: With grey, join pieces 7 and 8 along top long edge. Overcast all edges with grey. Glue roof to Wall Unit. Glue door overhang just above door, holding in place with pins until glue dries.

STEEPLE UNIT: Overcast openings on steeple sides and join pieces 9, 10, 11 and 12 with white. Overcast bottom and top edges with white. For steeple roof, join pieces 13, 14, 15 and 16 with grey along shaped sides. Overcast bottom edge with grey. Optional: With grey yarn, hang bell from inside the roof section. Tie yarn to bell at desired position. Glue steeple roof to steeple sides.

FENCE AND YARD: Join fence pieces 17, 18, 19 and 20 and overcast top edge with grey. Join fence to outer edge of yard (21) with grey. Overcast remaining edges of yard with white.

Finishing

Glue church to yard. Decorate as desired.

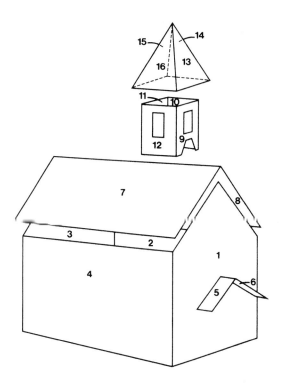

① FRONT (make 1)

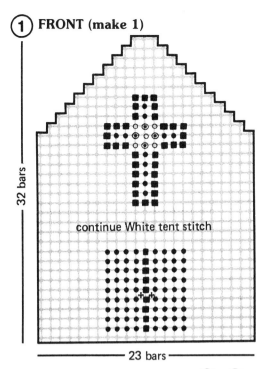

continue White tent stitch

32 bars

23 bars

③ BACK (make 1)

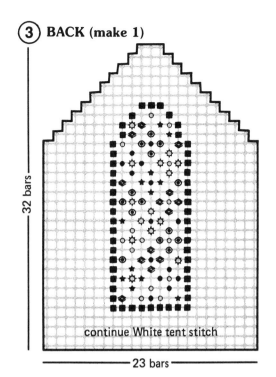

continue White tent stitch

32 bars

23 bars

COLOR KEY

- ⊹ = White tent stitch
- ○ = Yellow tent stitch
- ☆ = Grey tent stitch
- ✿ = Orange tent stitch
- ● = Red tent stitch
- ◉ = Green tent stitch
- ★ = Bright Blue tent stitch
- ⬢ = Purple tent stitch
- ■ = Black tent stitch
- / = White pattern stitch
- / = Grey pattern stitch
- + = Yellow French knot

② ④ SIDE (make 2)

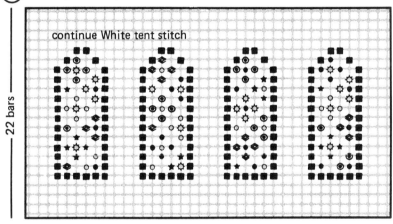

continue White tent stitch

22 bars

39 bars

⑤ ⑥ DOOR OVERHANG (make 2)

4 bars

11 bars

⑦ ⑧ ROOF (make 2)

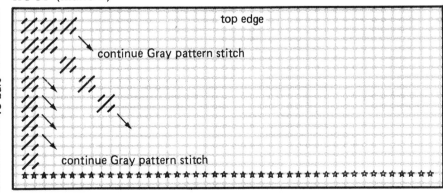

top edge

continue Gray pattern stitch

continue Gray pattern stitch

19 bars

46 bars

(Pattern charts continue on next page)

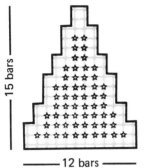

㉝ ㉕ ㉖ ㉗
STEEPLE ROOF (make 4)

15 bars
12 bars

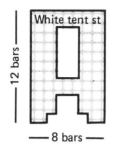

⑨ ⑪ **STEEPLE FRONT/BACK**
(make 2)

White tent st
12 bars
— 8 bars —

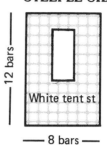

⑩ ⑫
STEEPLE SIDES (make 2)

White tent st
12 bars
— 8 bars —

COLOR KEY

✛	=	White tent stitch
○	=	Yellow tent stitch
✿	=	Grey tent stitch
✿	=	Orange tent stitch
●	=	Red tent stitch
◉	=	Green tent stitch
★	=	Bright Blue tent stitch
✿	=	Purple tent stitch
■	=	Black tent stitch
╱	=	White pattern stitch
╱	=	Grey pattern stitch
✛	=	Yellow French knot

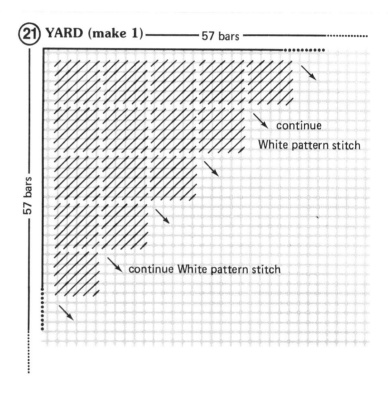

㉑ **YARD (make 1)** —— 57 bars ——

57 bars

continue
White pattern stitch

continue White pattern stitch

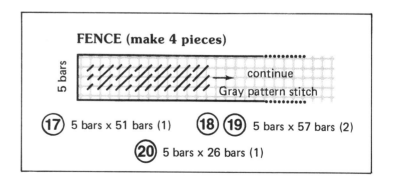

FENCE (make 4 pieces)

5 bars

continue
Gray pattern stitch

⑰ 5 bars x 51 bars (1)   ⑱ ⑲ 5 bars x 57 bars (2)

⑳ 5 bars x 26 bars (1)

CHRISTMAS CHURCH, *page 61*

NATIVITY GROUPING, *page 86*

CHRISTMAS TREES PLACEMATS & NAPKINS, *page 19*

CHRISTMAS TREE STOCKING, *page 91*

CHRISTMAS ANGEL ORNAMENTS, *page 96*
MR. & MRS. CLAUS ORNAMENTS, *page 104*

CHRISTMAS PILLOWS, *page 13* / CHRISTMAS TOTE BAG, *page 21*
SPINNING TRIANGLES TREE SKIRT, *page 25* / CHRISTMAS STOCKING, *page 23*

NATIVITY SET, *page 100*

JINGLE TREE CHRISTMAS
DECORATION, *page 123*

CHRISTMAS PARTY TABLE DECORATIONS, *page 54*

CROCHETED SNOWFLAKES, *page 117*

TREE-TOP ANGEL, *page 113*

CHRISTMAS COTTAGE, *page 46* / SANTA CENTERPIECE, *page 51*
LITTLE TRUNK GIFT BOX, *page 40* / CHRISTMAS PLACEMAT, COASTER & NAPKIN RING, *page 37*

CANDLEWICK CHRISTMAS TREE ORNAMENTS, *page 136*

CHRISTMAS STOCKINGS, *page 125*

MINI CHRISTMAS STOCKINGS, *page 115*

CROCHETED CHRISTMAS TABLE TREE, *page 121*

76

THE LITTLE LOG CABIN IN THE WOODS, *page 42*

CROCHETED PINEAPPLE ORNAMENT, *page 119*

POMPON SANTA, *page 30* / POMPON CHRISTMAS TREE, *page 31*

78

CANDLEWICK SNOWFLAKES, *page 138*

CANDLEWICK MINI CHRISTMAS WREATHS, *page 141*

79

CHRISTMAS AROUND THE WORLD
WALL HANGING, *page 97*

CHRISTMAS TREE WITH DIMENSIONAL
ORNAMENTS, *page 94*

COUNTED CROSS STITCH

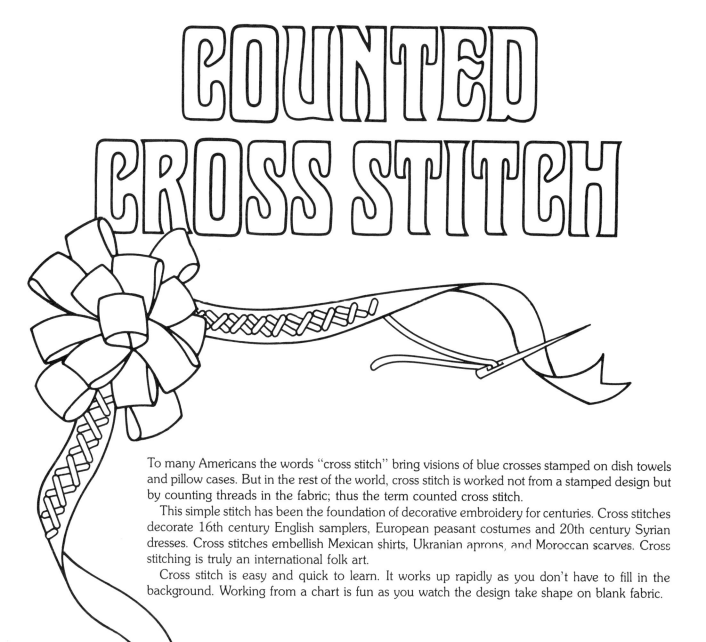

To many Americans the words "cross stitch" bring visions of blue crosses stamped on dish towels and pillow cases. But in the rest of the world, cross stitch is worked not from a stamped design but by counting threads in the fabric; thus the term counted cross stitch.

This simple stitch has been the foundation of decorative embroidery for centuries. Cross stitches decorate 16th century English samplers, European peasant costumes and 20th century Syrian dresses. Cross stitches embellish Mexican shirts, Ukranian aprons, and Moroccan scarves. Cross stitching is truly an international folk art.

Cross stitch is easy and quick to learn. It works up rapidly as you don't have to fill in the background. Working from a chart is fun as you watch the design take shape on blank fabric.

COUNTED CROSS STITCH HOW-TO

The materials required for counted cross stitch are few and inexpensive: a piece of evenweave fabric, a tapestry needle, some 6-strand cotton floss, and a charted design. An embroidery hoop is optional. All of these are readily available at most needlework shops.

EVENWEAVE FABRICS

These are designed especially for embroidery, and are woven with the same number of vertical and horizontal threads per inch. Cross stitches are made over the intersections of the horizontal and vertical threads, and because the number of threads in each direction is equal, each stitch will be the same size and perfectly square.

The evenweave fabrics most commonly used for cross stitch are:

AIDA CLOTH: A basketweave fabric in which horizontal and vertical threads are grouped, making the intersections for stitches very easy to see. Aida is woven with the intersections spaced in three different sizes: 11 count (11 stitches to the inch); 14 count (14 stitches to the inch) and 18 count (18 stitches to the inch).

The number of stitches per inch of any evenweave fabric determines the size of a design after it is worked. The photos in **Fig 1** show the same heart design worked on all three sizes of Aida. The more stitches to the inch, the smaller the design will be. Thus a design stitched on 18 count fabric will be considerably smaller than one stitched on 11 count fabric.

HARDANGER CLOTH: Woven with pairs of vertical and horizontal threads, the intersections in Hardanger are visible but not as pronounced as in Aida. All Hardanger is

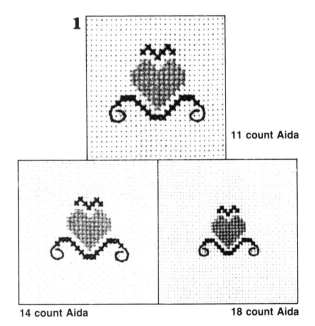

1

11 count Aida

14 count Aida　　　　**18 count Aida**

22 count fabric (22 stitches to the inch) which makes the stitches very small and delicate (**Fig 2**). Working on Hardanger becomes easier with practice.

2

**22 count
Hardanger**

Both Hardanger and Aida cloth are available in a wide range of lovely colors, but ivory and white are the ones most often used.

Evenweave fabrics are usually sold by the yard, half yard or cut in pieces. The per-yard price may seem expensive but a quarter of a yard provides enough fabric for many cross stitch projects.

HOOPS

Counted cross stitch can be done with or without a hoop. If you choose to stretch the fabric in a hoop, use one made of plastic or wood with a screw type tension adjuster. You may use a hoop large enough to accommodate the whole design or choose a small hoop, whichever you prefer. Placing the small hoop over existing stitches will slightly distort them but a gentle raking with the needle will restore their square shape. Be sure to remove the fabric from the hoop when you have finished stitching for the day.

If you are going to use a hoop, center it on the fabric with the tension screw at 10 o'clock if you are right handed, or at 2 o'clock if you are left handed. Pull fabric taut and tighten screw.

NEEDLES

Cross stitch is done with a blunt-pointed tapestry needle. The needle slips between the threads, not through them. **Fig 3** will tell you which size needle is appropriate for each kind of fabric.

FLOSS

Any six-strand cotton embroidery floss can be used for cross stitch. The six-strand floss can be divided to work with one, two or three strands as required by the fabric. **Fig 3** tells how many floss strands to use with the various fabrics.

3

FABRIC	STITCHES PER INCH	STRANDS OF FLOSS	TAPESTRY NEEDLE SIZE
Aida	11	3	24
Aida	14	2	24, 25 or 26
Aida	18	1 or 2	24, 25 or 26
Hardanger	22	1	24, 25 or 26

From the skein of floss, pull out an 18″ length and cut it off. Divide the 6 strands into 2 separate groups of 3 strands each. Thread 3 strands into the tapestry needle. Set needle and thread aside.

SCISSORS

A pair of small, sharp-pointed scissors is necessary, especially for snipping misplaced stitches. You may want to hang your scissors on a chain or ribbon around your neck—you'll need them often.

CHARTS

Counted cross stitch designs are worked from charts. Each square on a chart represents one cross stitch. The *symbol* in each square represents the floss color to be used. Narrow rules over or between symbols indicate back stitches. Each chart is accompanied by a color key, which gives the number of the suggested colors for either DMC Six Strand Floss or J. & P. Coats Deluxe Six Strand Floss. You may substitute with a comparable brand of 6-strand floss, pearl cotton or yarn. Each chart also gives you the number of stitches in width, then height of the design area.

Charts can be foolers: *the size of the charted design is not necessarily the size that your finished work will be.* The work size is determined by the number of *threads per inch* of the fabric you select. For example, if you work a motif that is 22 stitches wide and 11 stitches high on 11-count Aida, the worked design will be 2″ wide and 1″ high. Worked on 22-count Hardanger, the same design will be 1″ wide and ½″ high. *Fig 4* shows how much fabric is required for designs under 100 stitches in either direction.

STITCHES

CROSS STITCH: A single cross stitch is formed in two motions. Following the numbering in *Fig 5*, bring threaded needle up at 1, down at 2, up at 3, down at 4, completing the stitch. When working on Aida cloth, *Fig 5*, your stitch will cover one "block" of fabric.

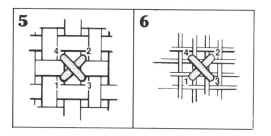

Hardanger has a simple weave and is described as having 22 threads per inch— it actually has 22 **pairs** of threads per inch. Work cross stitches over each intersection, *Fig 6*, to produce 22 stitches per inch. Be sure to use the "stab stitch" method (pull thread completely through fabric after each entry of the needle) rather than a "sewing" method to form cross stitches.

Work horizontal rows of stitches, *Fig 7*, whenever possible. Bring thread up at 1, holding tail end of thread beneath fabric and anchoring it with your first few stitches. Bring thread down at 2; repeat to end of row, forming first half of each stitch. Complete the stitches (3-4, 3-4) on the return journey right to left. Work second and subsequent rows below first row.

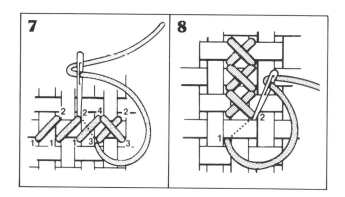

4

FABRIC	NUMBER OF STITCHES IN DESIGN									
	10	20	30	40	50	60	70	80	90	100
11 AIDA	1″	2″	2¾″	3¾″	4½″	5½″	6½″	7¼″	8¼″	9″
14 AIDA	¾″	1½″	2¼″	2¾″	3½″	4¼″	5″	5¾″	6½″	7¼″
18 AIDA	½″	1¼″	1½″	2¼″	2¾″	3½″	4″	4½″	5″	5½″
HARDANGER	½″	1″	1½″	2″	2¼″	2¾″	3¼″	3¾″	5″	4½″

Measurements given to next larger quarter inch.

When a vertical row of stitches is appropriate, complete each stitch then proceed to the next, *Fig 8*. No matter how you work the stitches, make sure that all crosses slant in the same direction.

End thread by running the needle over and under several stitches on the wrong side of fabric; begin new threads in this manner if stitches are available. Trim thread ends close to fabric. Because knots in embroidery cause lumps that show under the fabric when it's framed or sewn into finished projects, never begin or end with a knot.

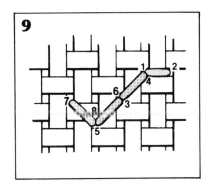

BACK STITCH: Back stitches are usually worked after cross stitches have been completed. They may slope in any direction and are occasionally worked over more than one fabric block or thread. *Fig 9* shows the progression of several stitches; bring thread up at odd numbers, down at even numbers.

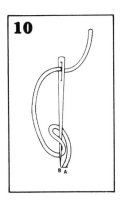

FRENCH KNOT: Work French knots by bringing thread to front of fabric at A, *Fig 10*. Wrap thread once around shaft of needle. Insert needle at B, next to A. Hold wrapped thread as needle is pulled through fabric, releasing it as knot is formed close to surface. For a larger knot, use several strands of floss; wrap around needle only once.

PLANNING A PROJECT

The designs in this book are shown finished as suggested Christmas projects. You may wish to use some of these cross stitch designs for other projects. Whichever project you work, select your chart and type of fabric. Next determine the finished dimensions of a stitched area. Divide the number of stitches in width by the number of stitches per inch of fabric. This tells you how many inches wide the fabric must be. Repeat for the height of the design.

Add enough additional fabric for unworked area around the design plus an additional 2″ all around for use in finishing and mounting. If your design is a small one, be sure to allow enough fabric to fit over your smallest hoop. The excess fabric can be cut off after stitching.

Cut your fabric exactly true, right along the holes of the fabric. Some ravelling will occur as you handle the fabric; however, an overcast basting stitch, machine zigzag stitch, or masking tape around the raw edges will minimize ravelling.

At bottom and sides of each chart are arrows or dots which indicate the center (which may be a row of stitches, or between two rows of stitches). Find the center of the fabric by folding it in half horizontally and then vertically. Baste along both fold lines; the basting (which is removed when stitching is completed) will cross at the middle and aid in counting stitches.

It is best to start stitching at the top of the design (or the top of a color area) and work downward, whenever possible. This way your needle comes up in an empty hole and goes down in a used hole. This makes your work look neater and is easier than bringing the needle up through an already occupied hole.

To begin stitching, count up from the center hole of the fabric to the top stitches indicated on the chart.

FINISHING

Cross stitch on any evenweave fabric is fully washable. When you have finished stitching, dampen embroidery (or wash in lukewarm mild soap suds if soiled and rinse well); roll it briefly in a clean towel to remove excess moisture. Place embroidery face down on a dry, clean terry towel and iron carefully until dry and smooth. Make sure all thread ends are well anchored and clipped closely. Then proceed with desired finishing.

Several of the projects shown can also be framed as pictures. For cross stitch to look its best in a frame it should be stretched taut over a piece of heavy cardboard with the following method of lacing. You will need white cardboard or mat board the size of your frame, 1 spool of white heavy duty sewing thread, pins and four strips of paper.

Step 1: Lay stitchery (washed and pressed) face up on table. Lay strips of paper about ½″ out from each side of design. Adjust paper until a pleasing border surrounds stitched area. Mark inside edge of paper strips with pins; remove paper. Measure horizontally and vertically between pins and cut board that size. (If you have a frame, cut board same size as glass.)

Step 2: Cut fabric about 3″ out from pins on all sizes.

Step 3: Place stitchery face down on table. Place cardboard within pins, aligning top edge of board with weave of fabric. Fold extra fabric toward you over cardboard; pin every ½" into edge of board (**Fig 11**). Follow weave while pinning to keep design straight. Pulling fabric taut, fold up bottom fabric and pin. Repeat on sides. Remove marking pins from fabric.

Step 4: Working off a spool of white sewing thread, thread a sharp needle. Beginning at right edge, make a small stitch on top hem, then a small stitch directly below in bottom hem. Now go back to top hem and make another small stitch about ½" from first; then back to bottom hem, pulling thread from spool through stitches as you go (**Fig 12**). Continue across, secure thread at top when you reach left edge of board. Cut needle off. Now, working backwards, pull every other lacing thread taut with right hand (hold stitch just tightened with left forefinger). When you reach right side, cut thread off spool, leaving 8" end. Re-thread needle and secure lacing thread. Remove pins. Repeat for sides.

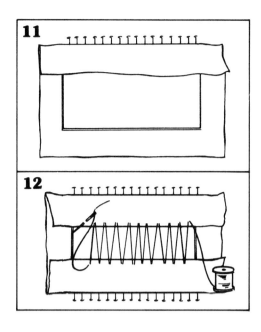

JOSEPH AND MARY

THREE KINGS

SHEPHERD SCENE

86

NATIVITY GROUPING

designed by Carol Wilson Mansfield

These three designs can be framed alone or used as part of a grouping. We show them framed in wooden hoops. This is an easy and attractive way to display designs. The hoops come in a wide range of sizes (6″, 8″, 10″, 12″, 14″ in diameter) and have an attractive wood finish that can be used as is, or painted to highlight the design using regular acrylic paints available in craft departments.

Size

8″ in diameter worked on 14-count Aida

Design Size

Joseph and Mary, 74 stitches wide × 89 stitches high
Three Kings, 78 stitches wide × 88 stitches high
Shepherd Scene, 63 stitches wide × 83 stitches high

Materials

14-count Aida cloth
6-strand embroidery floss:

J. & P. COATS

81A	Colonial Brown
51C	Gold Brown
260	Maple Wood
124	Indian Pink
38	Dk. Orange
24B	Dk. Oriental Blue
132A	Parakeet
98	Fern Green
71	Pewter Grey
32	Purple
100	Fast Red
140	Signal Red

Three 8″ in diameter wood hoops
1 yd white fabric
Quilt batting (*optional*)
White felt (*optional*)

Instructions

Work design centered on 12″ × 12″ fabric. Wash and press finished piece.

Finishing

Step 1: Place stitched piece wrong side up on flat surface, and center outer ring of chosen hoop over design. With pencil, lightly draw around the hoop. Now measure and draw a 2″ allowance all around circle. Remove hoop, pin stitched piece to piece of white lining fabric, then cut out both fabrics at same time along allowance line. (*NOTE: You may if you wish add a thin layer of quilt batting to be sandwiched between stitched piece and lining.*)

Step 2: If you plan to paint hoop, do it now. Paint only outer ring of hoop. You will probably need to apply one coat, let it dry, then a second coat. Be sure paint is completely dry before proceeding. Do not paint metal screw.

Step 3: Place inner ring of hoop on flat surface. Place outer ring on top of fabric, slide down over inner ring. Adjust screw to hold work taut, pulling fabric as necessary to eliminate wrinkles.

Step 4: Turn project to back side; with needle and sewing thread, run a gathering line through all fabric layers around outer edge of work, about ¼″ in from outer fabric edge. Pull up gathers so that work lies flat in back. Secure thread firmly. If desired, a felt circle can be glued to back of piece to hide gathered area.

JOSEPH AND MARY

COLOR KEY

		J. & P. Coats				J. & P. Coats
■	=	81A	Colonial Brown	★	=	38 Dk. Orange
◉	=	51C	Gold Brown	◈	=	24B Dk. Oriental Blue
○	=	260	Maple Wood	•	=	132A Parakeet
·	=	124	Indian Pink	+	=	98 Fern Green

THREE KINGS

COLOR KEY

		J. & P. Coats				J. & P. Coats	
■	=	81A	Colonial Brown	·	=	124	Indian Pink
⊚	=	51C	Gold Brown	★	=	38	Dk. Orange
○	=	260	Maple Wood	✎	=	24B	Dk. Oriental Blue
✦	=	32	Purple	●	=	132A	Parakeet
◢	=	100	Fast Red	+	=	98	Fern Green
◦	=	140	Signal Red	∧	=	71	Pewter Grey

(Pattern charts continue on next page)

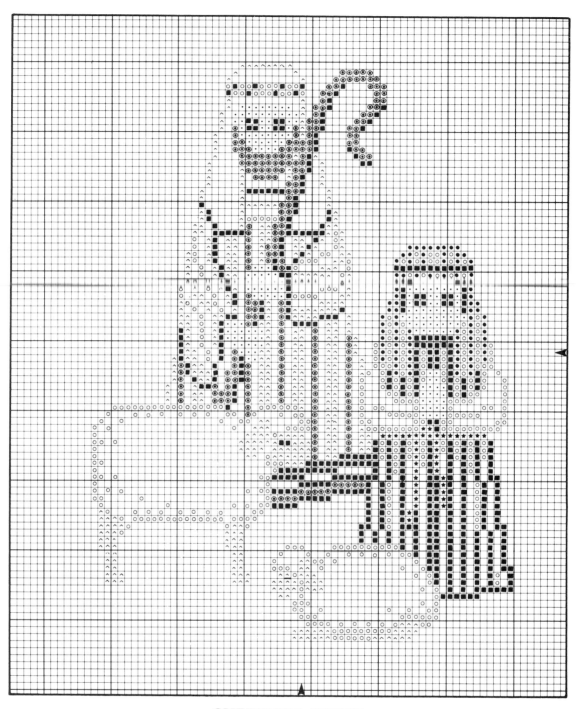

SHEPHERD SCENE

COLOR KEY

		J. & P. Coats				J. & P. Coats	
■	=	81A	Colonial Brown	★	=	38	Dk. Orange
◉	=	51C	Gold Brown	•	=	132A	Parakeet
○	=	260	Maple Wood	^	=	71	Pewter Grey
·	=	124	Indian Pink				

CHRISTMAS TREE
STOCKING

designed by Louise O'Donnell

The whole family—including grandma and the family pet—is decorating the Christmas tree. And the whole scene is decorating this charming Christmas stocking. Make several and vary the size by using different fabric.

Size

19¼″ × 9½″ worked on 11-count Aida
15″ × 7½″ worked on 14-count Aida
11¾″ × 6″ worked on 18-count Aida
9½″ × 4¾″ worked on Hardanger

Design Size

211 stitches long × 105 stitches wide

Materials

Choice of fabric
6-strand embroidery floss:

DMC	
414	Dk. Grey
898	V. Dk. Coffee Brown
799	Lt. Blue
413	Dk. Grey
816	Crimson
996	Med. Blue
699	Dk. Green
666	Red
782	Dk. Gold
754	Flesh
792	Dk. Cornflower Blue
444	Yellow
906	Lt. Green

Lining Fabric
Backing Fabric

(NOTE: Top of chart is on page 92; bottom of chart is on page 93.)

Instructions

Following chart, stitch design, centering it carefully on large square of fabric. Wash and press finished piece.

Finishing

Step 1: Stay-stitch intended seamline (black line on chart). Cut out stocking allowing a ½″ seam allowance.

Step 2: Using cross stitch as pattern, cut two stockings from lining fabric and one from backing fabric.

Step 3: Right sides together, join backing to embroidery, sewing down the sides and along bottom of foot. Clip where necessary along curve. **Do not turn the stocking right side out.**

Step 4: Right sides together, join two lining pieces, sewing them down sides and along bottom of foot. Clip where necessary along curve. **Turn right side out.**

Step 5: Right sides together, carefully place lining into stocking. Match seams. Carefully stitch across ½″ seam allowance at top of stocking, leaving an opening large enough for turning. Turn right side out and tuck lining into stocking. Fold under unfinished seam allowances and slip stitch lining to stocking. Add trim along top if desired.

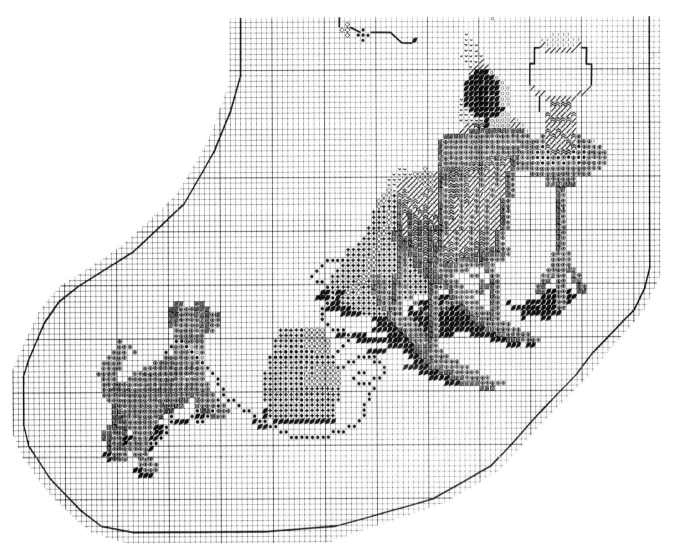

COLOR KEY

		DMC				DMC	
○	=	414	Dk. Grey	•	=	666	Red
⋒	=	898	V. Dk. Coffee Brown	◉	=	782	Dk. Gold
⁄	=	799	Lt. Blue	-	=	754	Flesh
◢	=	413	Dk. Grey	≫	=	792	Dk. Cornflower Blue
▼	=	816	Crimson	˒	=	444	Yellow
×	=	996	Med blue	◇	=	906	Lt. Green
+	=	699	Dk. Green	413	–	Dk. Grey; backstitch on string of lights	
				898	=	V. Dk. Coffee Brown, backstitch girl's eyelash	
				799	=	Lt. Blue; backstitch around lamp	

CHRISTMAS TREE WITH DIMENSIONAL ORNAMENTS

designed by Carol Wilson Mansfield

This may seem like just another Christmas tree picture, but look closely. The two ornaments are dimensional motifs that almost jump out from the picture frame.

Size

8″ × 8″ worked on Hardanger (*22*) over two threads

Design Size

87 stitches wide × 89 stitches high

Materials

22-count Hardanger
6-strand embroidery floss:

DMC

677	Cream
729	Gold
781	Dk Gold
907	Lime Green
989	Medium Green
319	Dk. Green
893	Pink
666	Bright Red
498	Dk. Red
309	Dk. Rose

Small piece iron-on interfacing
Small piece muslin
Small amount polyester fiberfill
8″ × 8″ foam core
8″ × 8″ frame

Instructions

Work main design centered on a piece of Hardanger fabric. Wash; press smooth according to instructions on page 84. Work ornaments on separate pieces of Hardanger. Wash; press smooth according to instructions on page 84.

Finishing

ORNAMENT: Place the fusing side of iron-on interfacing over the *wrong* side of each ornament. Trace outline of design with pencil; cut interfacing along this line. Fuse to wrong side of work following manufacturer's directions.

Place a piece of muslin (or other finely-woven lining fabric) beneath embroidery, right sides together. Machine-stitch (fine setting) completely around ornament, using edge of interfacing as well as edge of design as your stitching guideline. Trim seam allowance to ⅛″.

Now, cut a small slit lengthwise in the lining fabric only; the slit will be an inch or less in length, just enough for turning. Use slit to turn piece right side out, making sure all curves are thoroughly, but carefully, turned. Press well. Insert a thin layer of fiberfill into ornament. Turn under raw edge of one side of slit and blindstitch by hand to opposite side. Closing the slit in this manner narrows the lining just enough to puff out the detached ornament.

PICTURE: Stretch embroidery over foam core. Attach ornament by tacking to front of embroidery according to placement noted on chart; tack through foam core and anchor on back. Insert into frame. If not using foam core, ornament may be tacked on before framing.

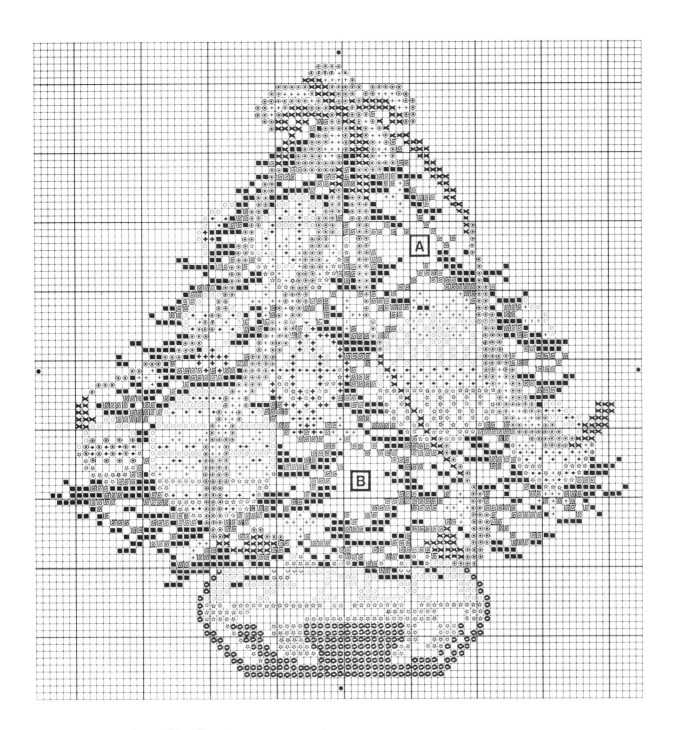

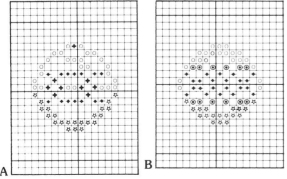

A

B

Attach two ornaments to Squares A and B

COLOR KEY

	DMC				DMC	
○ =	677	Cream		■ =	319	Dk. Green
☆ =	729	Gold		+ =	893	Pink
◕ −	781	Dk. Gold		◉ =	666	Bright Red
◆ =	907	Lime Green		✕ =	498	Dk. Red
⌑ =	989	Med. Green		✦ =	309	Dk. Rose

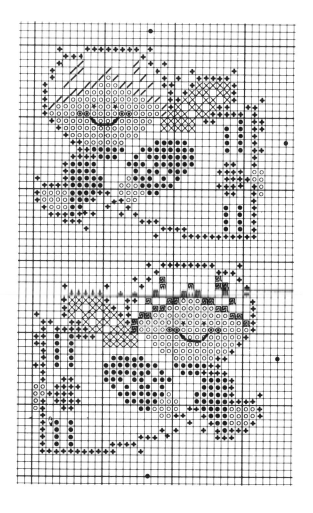

COLOR KEY

	DMC				DMC	
+	=	666 Red		○	=	818 Lt. Pink
╱	=	444 Yellow		◉	=	957 Pink
●	=	701 Green		×	=	741 Yellow-Orange
⬒	=	975 Brown		★	=	517 Blue
	Smiles	=	957	Backstitches		

CHRISTMAS ANGEL ORNAMENTS

designed by Anis Duncan

These pixie-like angels are finished like tiny pincushions and then hung on your Christmas tree. They could also be framed like the Mr. and Mrs. Claus ornaments on page 104.

Size

Approx 2½″ × 2″ worked on 14-Aida

Design Size

33 sts wide × 27 sts long

Materials

14-count Aida cloth
6-strand embroidery floss:
   DMC
   666   Red
   444   Yellow
   701   Green
   975   Brown

818   Lt. Pink
957   Pink
741   Yellow-Orange
517   Blue
⅛ yd backing fabric
½ yd ruffled lace edging
Small amount polyester fiberfill

Instructions

Work design. Wash and press according to instructions on page 84.

Finishing

Measure ¾″ out from stitching all around. Cut along this line. Cut backing fabric same size. Baste lace edging to right side of stitchery with fullness toward center and gathered edge ½″ from cut edge of fabric. Baste backing on top, right sides together. Stitch ⅝″ seam around, leaving 1″ open. Clip and trim seam; turn. Insert small amount of polyester stuffing. Blind stitch opening.

CHRISTMAS
AROUND THE WORLD
WALL HANGING

designed by Carol Wilson Mansfield

Christmas celebrated around the world is depicted in this wall hanging in which the traditional Christmas greeting is expressed in English, Spanish, French and Italian.

Size

8½″ × 17″ worked on 14-count Aida

Design Size

102 stitches wide × 215 stitches high

Materials

13″ × 20″ piece 14-count ivory or white Aida
13″ × 20″ piece red or green calico backing fabric
8½″ × ⅜″ diameter dowel rod
2 upholstery length gold thumb tacks
12″ piece gold metallic chain
6-strand embroidery floss

J & P COATS

240	Nasturtium
48A	Dk. Hunter's Green
48	Hunter's Green
54	Violet
132A	Parakeet

(NOTE: Top of chart is on page 98; bottom of chart is on page 99.)

Instructions

Work design centered on fabric. Wash and press finished piece. On wrong side of piece, measure and mark a line 2″ above top row of stitching (top of "M" on word "Merry"); and 2″ below last row of stitching (bottom of "t" on word "Natale"). Measure and mark a line 1¼″ out from last "s" in word "Christmas," and on other side, mark a line 1¼″ out from "C" of word "Christmas". Trim along these lines. This gives you a ½″ seam allowance all around.

Finishing

Step 1: Cut a 13″ × 20″ piece of red or green calico backing fabric to exact size of stitched piece.

Step 2: Pin stitched piece and backing together, wrong sides facing.

Step 3: With ½″ seam allowance, sew across top of piece.

Step 4: For rod opening, drop down ⅜″ from top seam, and sew one side seam and along part of bottom leaving a 4″ opening at bottom for turning inside out. Start again on other side of opening, and sew rest of bottom, then up opposite side to within ⅜″ of top seam.

Step 5: Trim seams, clip corners, turn right side out. Slip stitch bottom opening closed. Press.

Step 6: At openings left for rod, be sure seam allowance is turned inside. Stitch across top ⅜″ below top edge for rod pocket.

Step 7: Insert 8½″ × ⅜″ diameter dowel rod in pocket. At each end, attach gold chain (we used a 12″ length) with gold upholstery length thumb tacks.

COLOR KEY

J. & P. Coats

■	=	240	Nasturtium
●	=	48A	Dk. Hunter's Green
○	=	48	Hunter's Green
+	=	54	Violet
★	=	132A	Parakeet

NATIVITY SET

designed by Carol Wilson Mansfield and Julie Ryan

This elegant six-piece Nativity set will look lovely sitting on your Christmas mantlepiece. You can also use these as hanging ornaments on your Christmas tree by attaching a loop of gold thread. We show the designs worked on white Hardanger. You might use colored fabrics and/ or metallic threads for attractive variations.

Size

4½″ tall worked on Hardanger 22 over two threads

Design Size

96 sts wide × 55 sts high

Materials

22-count Hardanger
6-strand embroidery floss:

DMC
800	Lt. Blue
996	Med. Blue
820	Dk. Blue
754	Flesh
838	Dk. Brown
742	Yellow
729	Gold
907	Lt. Green
321	Red
975	Lt. Brown
413	Dk. Grey
3072	Lt. Grey
318	Med. Grey

DMC
844	Dk. Grey
435	Lt. Rust
300	Rust
839	Dk. Brown
552	Purple
310	Black
700	Med. Green
895	Dk. Green
995	Med-Dk. Blue

Lining fabric
Iron-on interfacing
Gold braid and cording

Instructions

Work design. Wash and press according to instructions on page 84.

Finishing

The dotted line around each design shows suggested seamline. Cut fabric ½″ beyond this line; cut one piece of stiff lining to match each embroidered piece. Adhere iron-on interfacing to the wrong side of each figure. With right sides together, sew lining to embroidery around upper and lower curved edges; leave ends open. Turn right side out and press again.

At each end, turn seam allowance to inside and hand-sew outer piece to lining. Blindstitch two ends together to form cone-shaped figure. Sew a length of gold braid around top edge of each King for crowns and gold cording around top of Mary and Joseph for halos.

MARY AND JESUS

COLOR KEY

DMC

× = 800   Lt. Blue

✦ = 996   Med. Blue

𝔫 = 820   Dk. Blue

+ = 754   Flesh

✖ = 838   Dk. Brown

○ = 742   Yellow

● = 729   Gold

♪ = 907   Lt. Green
            (backstitch)

╱ = 321   Red
            (backstitch)

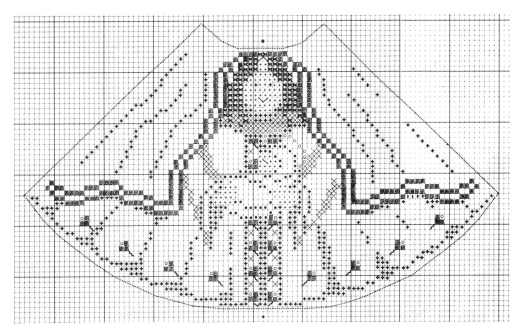

JOSEPH

COLOR KEY

DMC

♠ = 838   Dk. Brown

● = 975   Lt. Brown

○ = 729   Gold

× = 907   Lt. Green

+ = 754   Flesh

⬟ = 413   Dk. Grey

╱ = 321   Red
            (backstitch)

(Pattern charts continue on next page)

SHEPHERD

COLOR KEY

DMC

×	=	3072	Lt. Grey
✦	=	318	Med. Grey
▣	=	844	Dk. Grey
○	=	435	Lt. Rust
✿	=	300	Rust
⫿	=	839	Dk. Brown
✦	=	996	Blue
◉	=	321	Red
+	=	754	Flesh

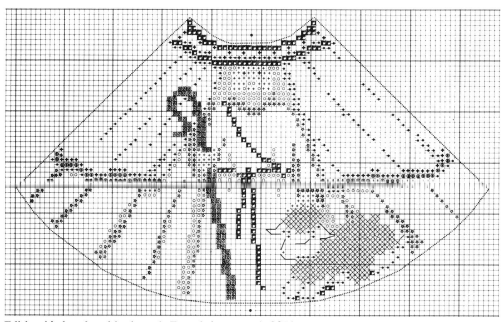

Fill lamb's head and body with French knots with 3072

WISEMAN

COLOR KEY

DMC

⅁	=	552	Purple
✦	=	435	Brown
○	=	729	Gold
×	=	742	Yellow
◉	=	321	Red
▣	=	310	Black

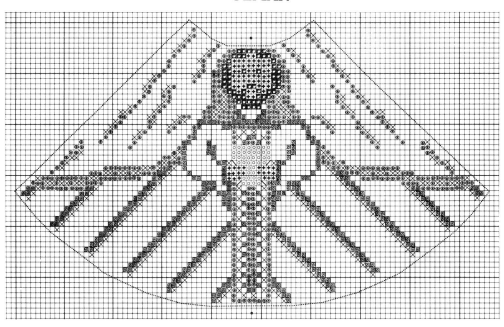

WISEMAN

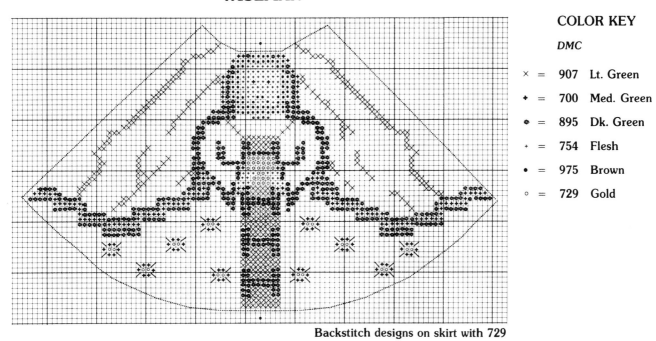

COLOR KEY

DMC

×	=	907	Lt. Green
✦	=	700	Med. Green
☙	=	895	Dk. Green
＋	=	754	Flesh
●	=	975	Brown
○	=	729	Gold

Backstitch designs on skirt with 729

WISEMAN

COLOR KEY

DMC

×	=	800	Lt. Blue
●	=	996	Med. Blue
✦	=	995	Med-Dk. Blue
▣	=	820	Navy Blue
＋	=	754	Flesh
○	=	729	Gold
▣	=	310	Black

Backstitches on lantern are 310

  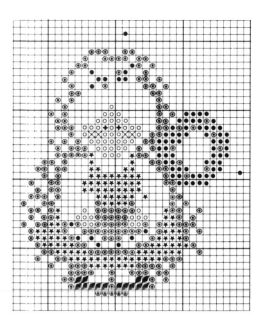

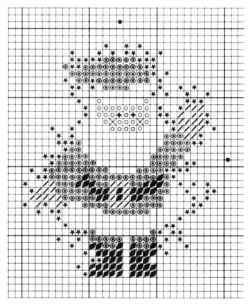

MR. AND MRS. CLAUS ORNAMENTS

designed by Anis Duncan

Santa and his wife will make a delightful pair of Christmas ornaments. The design works up very quickly, and they are framed in a ready-made gold frame. They can also be finished as little pincushions like the angels on page 96.

Size

3″ in diameter worked on 18-Aida

Design Size

Mrs. Santa, 31 sts wide × 36 sts high
Santa, 29 sts wide × 34 sts high

Materials

18-count Aida cloth
6-strand embroidery floss:

    DMC

      666   Red
      701   Green
      699   Dk. Green
      818   Lt. Pink
      741   Yellow-Orange
      517   Blue
      310   Black
      957   Pink
Frame

Instructions

Work design. Wash and press according to instructions on page 84.

Finishing

Frame in 3″ frame.

COLOR KEY

DMC

◉	=	666	Red
＊	=	701	Green
●	=	699	Dk. Green
○	=	818	Lt. Pink
╱	=	741	Yellow-Orange
✦	=	517	Blue
◢	=	310	Black
×	=	957	Pink

CROCHETING & KNITTING

With crochet hook and knitting needle, what charming Christmas ornaments, decorations and gifts you can create! In this chapter you'll find decorations for your Christmas table, ornaments to hang on your tree, as well as Christmas stockings for every member of the family.

CROCHETING AND KNITTING HOW-TO

CROCHETING

Chain (ch)

Crochet always starts with a basic chain. To begin, make a slip loop on hook (**Fig 1**), leaving a 4″ tail of yarn.

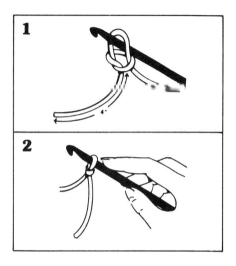

Step 1: Take hook in right hand, holding it between thumb and third finger (**Fig 2**), and rest index finger near tip of hook.

Step 2: Take slip loop in thumb and index finger of left hand (**Fig 3**) and bring yarn over third finger of left hand, catching it loosely at left palm with remaining two fingers.

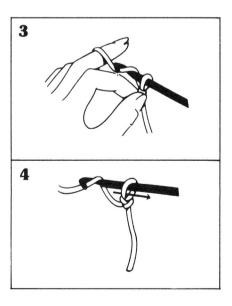

Step 3: Bring yarn over hook from back to front (**Fig 4**), and draw through loop on hook.

One chain made. Repeat Step 3 for each additional chain desired, moving your left thumb and index finger up close to the hook after each stitch or two (**Fig 5**).

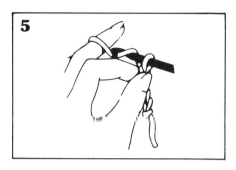

When counting number of chains, do not count the loop on the hook or the starting slip knot.

Single Crochet (sc)

First, make a chain to desired length.

Step 1: Insert hook in top loop of 2nd chain from hook (**Fig 6**); hook yarn (bring yarn over hook from back to front) and draw through (**Fig 7**).

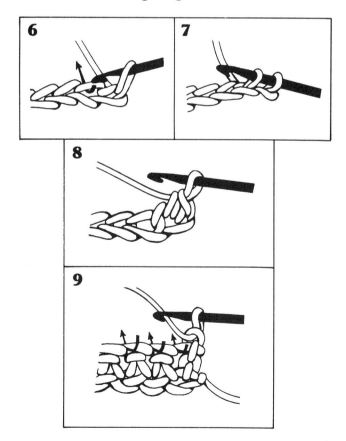

Step 2: Hook yarn and draw through 2 loops on hook (*Fig 8*).

One single crochet made. Work a single crochet (repeat Steps 1 and 2) in each remaining chain.

To work additional rows, chain 1 and turn work counterclockwise. Inserting hook under 2 loops of the stitch (*Fig 9*), work a single crochet (as before) in each stitch across.

Double Crochet (dc)

Double crochet is a taller stitch than single crochet. Begin by making a chain to desired length.

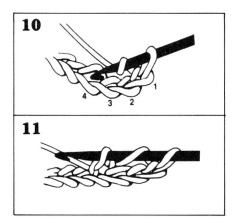

Step 1: Bring yarn once over the hook; insert hook in the top loop of the 4th chain from hook (*Fig 10*). Hook yarn and draw through (*Fig 11*).

Step 2: Hook yarn and draw through first 2 loops on hook (*Fig 12*).

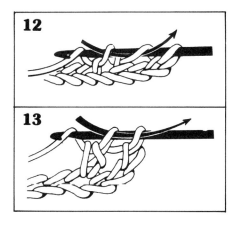

Step 3: Hook yarn and draw through last 2 loops on hook (*Fig 13*).

One double crochet made. Work a double crochet (repeat Steps 1 through 3) in each remaining chain.

To work additional rows, make 3 chains and turn work counterclockwise. Beginning in 2nd stitch (*Fig 14*—3

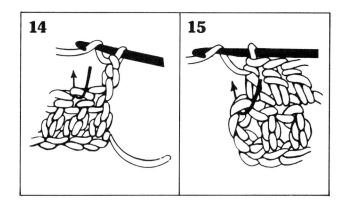

chains count as first double crochet), work a double crochet (as before) in each stitch across (remember to insert hook under 2 top loops of stitch). At end of row, work last double crochet in the top chain of chain-3 (*Fig 15*).

Half Double Crochet (hdc)

This stitch eliminates one step of double crochet—hence its name. It is taller than single crochet, but shorter than double crochet. Begin by making a chain to desired length.

Step 1: Bring yarn over hook; insert hook in top loop of 3rd chain from hook, hook yarn and draw through (3 loops now on hook).

Step 2: Hook yarn and draw through all 3 loops on hook (*Fig 16*).

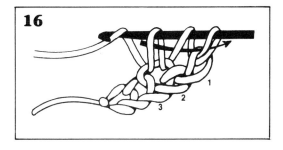

One half double crochet made. Work a half double crochet (repeat Steps 1 and 2) in each remaining chain.

To work additional rows, make 2 chains and turn work counterclockwise. Beginning in 2nd stitch (2 chains count as first half double crochet), work a half double crochet (as before) in each stitch across. At end of row, work last half double crochet in the top chain of chain-2.

Triple Crochet (tr)

Triple crochet is a tall stitch that works up quickly. First, make a chain to desired length.

Step 1: Bring yarn twice over the hook, insert hook in 5th chain from hook (*Fig 17*); hook yarn and draw through (*Fig 18*).

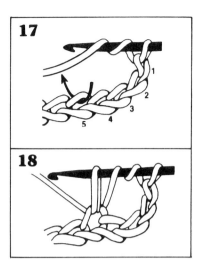

Step 2: Hook yarn and draw through first 2 loops on hook (*Fig 19*).

Step 3: Hook yarn and draw through next 2 loops on hook (*Fig 20*).

Step 4: Hook yarn and draw through remaining 2 loops on hook (*Fig 21*).

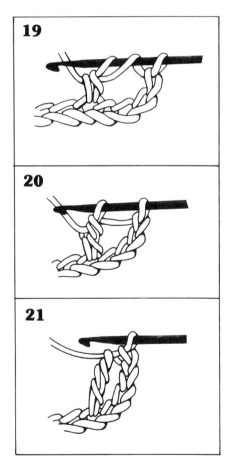

One triple crochet made. Work a triple crochet (repeat Steps 1 through 4) in each remaining chain.

To work additional rows, make 4 chains and turn work counterclockwise. Beginning in 2nd stitch (4 chains count as first triple crochet), work a triple crochet (as before) in each stitch across. At end of row, work last triple crochet in the top chain of chain-4.

Slip Stitch (sl st)

This is the shortest of all crochet stitches, and usually is used to join work, or to move yarn across a group of stitches without adding height. To practice, make a chain to desired length; then work one row of double crochets.

Step 1: Insert hook in first st; hook yarn and draw through both stitch and loop on hook in one motion (*Fig 22*).

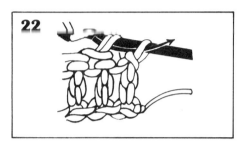

One slip stitch made. Work a slip stitch (repeat Step 1) in each stitch across.

CROCHETING WITH THREAD AND A STEEL HOOK

Don't be afraid to crochet with steel hooks and finer thread. You will be using exactly the same stitches you're familiar with, but at first it will feel clumsy and awkward. For an experienced crocheter, this is a bit of a surprise—suddenly feeling all thumbs again just as when you first learned to crochet. But this will pass in a few hours of crocheting, as you adjust your tension and working method to the new tools. Soon you will work much more by feel than when working with the heavier yarns. So be patient with any initial clumsiness and confusion—they won't be with you long.

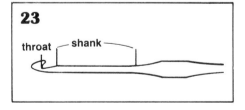

Steel hooks range in size from 00 (large) to 14 (very fine), and are 5″ long which is shorter than the aluminum or plastic hooks. Their shape is different from the other crochet hooks. There is the throat, then the shank, and after the shank the steel begins to widen again before it reaches the finger grip (*Fig 23*). When crocheting, it is important that the stitches do not slide beyond the shank as this will cause a loose tension and alter the gauge. If you find you are having difficulty at first, put a piece of cellophane tape around the hook to keep the stitches from sliding past the correct area. With practice, you will work in the right place automatically.

WASHING: If your finished project should need washing, use warm water and a mild soap. Wash gently; do not rub, twist or wring. Rinse well, and gently press water out of piece. Roll piece up in a terry towel, then lay it out to dry as explained in the following blocking instructions.

BLOCKING: This simply means "setting" the finished piece into its final size and shape. To do this, spread the piece out on a flat padded surface (covered with terry toweling), having wrong side facing up. Be sure to shape piece to measurements given with the pattern, having picots, loops, scallops, etc. along the outside edges open and in correct alignment. If necessary, use rust-proof straight pins to hold the edges in place. If piece was not previously washed, dampen it thoroughly with a wet sponge or cloth, or spray it with a commercial spray starch—this will give a firmer shape but not stiff. Let dry completely before removing.

If further blocking is necessary, press through a damp cloth with a moderately hot iron on the wrong side (do not rest iron on any decorative raised stitch). When thoroughly dried, remove.

STARCHING: If a stiff finish is required, use a solution of a commercial boilable starch (spray starches won't do the job), or a sugar-and-water starch that was traditionally used for old-fashioned doilies.

Sugar-and-Water Starch: Mix ½ cup each of granulated sugar and water in a small pan; heat to a rapid boil. Immediately remove from heat; cool to room temperature. Immerse finished piece in starch until thoroughly saturated. Remove from starch (don't wring—piece should be very wet). Block out to specified shape as previously explained, and let dry thoroughly (this may even take several days in muggy weather).

KNITTING

Casting On (CO)

Only one knitting needle is used with this method. First, measure off a length of yarn that allows about 1″ for each stitch you are going to cast on. Make a slip knot on needle as follows. Make a yarn loop, leaving about 4″ length of yarn at free end; insert needle into loop and draw up yarn from free end to make a loop on needle (**Fig 24**). Pull yarn firmly, but not tightly, to form a slip knot on needle (**Fig 25**). This slip knot counts as your first stitch. Now work as follows.

Step 1: Hold needle with slip knot in right hand, with yarn from skein to your right, and measured length of yarn to your left. With left hand, make a yarn loop (**Fig 26**) and insert needle into loop (**Fig 27**).

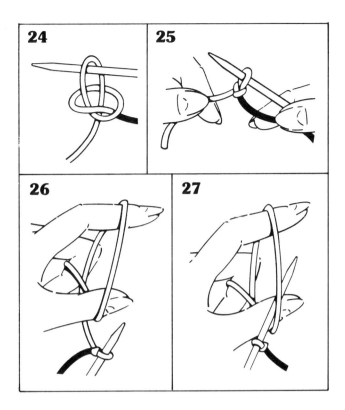

Step 2: Still holding loop in left hand; with right hand, pick up yarn from skein and bring it from back to front around the needle (**Fig 28**).

Step 3: Bring needle through loop and toward you; at the same time, pull gently on yarn end to tighten loop (**Fig 29**). Make it snug but not tight below needle.

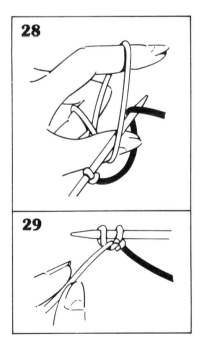

You now have one cast-on stitch. Repeat Steps 1 through 3 for each additional stitch desired.

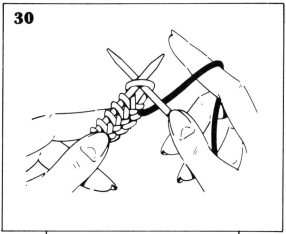

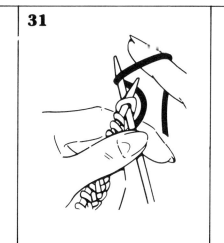

The Knit Stitch (K)

Step 1: Hold the needle with cast-on stitches in your left hand. Insert point of right needle in first stitch, from left to right, just as in casting on (**Fig 30**).

Step 2: With right index finger, bring yarn under and over point of right needle (**Fig 31**).

Step 3: Draw yarn through stitch with right needle point (**Fig 32**).

Step 4: Slip the loop on the left needle off, so the new stitch is entirely on the right needle (**Fig 33**).

This completes one knit stitch.

The Purl Stitch (P)

The reverse of the knit stitch is called the purl stitch. Instead of inserting the right needle point from left to right under the left needle (as you did for the knit stitch), you will now insert it from right to left, in front of the left needle.

Step 1: Insert right needle, from right to left, into first stitch, and in front of left needle (**Fig 34**).

Step 2: Holding yarn in front of work (side toward you), bring it around right needle counterclockwise (**Fig 35**).

Step 3: With right needle, pull yarn back through stitch (**Fig 36**). Slide stitch off left needle, leaving new stitch on right needle (**Fig 37**).

One purl stitch is now completed.

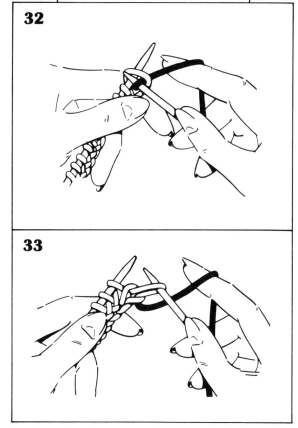

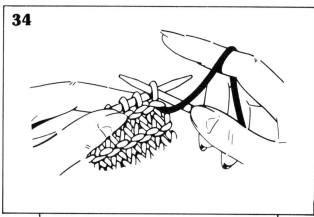

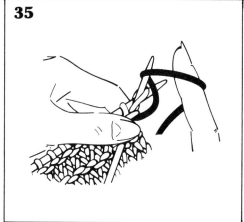

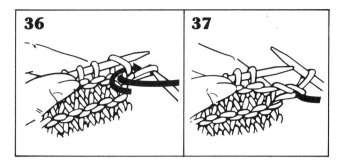

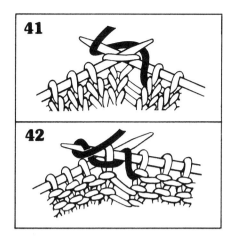

Binding Off (BO)

To bind off on the knit side:

Step 1: Knit the first 2 stitches. Then insert left needle into the first of the 2 stitches (*Fig 38*), and pull it over the second stitch and completely off the needle (*Fig 39*). You have now bound off one stitch.

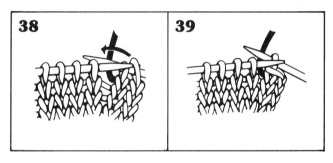

Step 2: Knit one more stitch; insert left needle into first stitch on right needle and pull it over the new stitch and completely off the needle (*Fig 40*). Another stitch is now bound off.

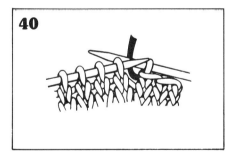

Repeat Step 2 until all sts are bound off and one loop remains on right-hand needle. "Finish off" or "end off" the yarn (cut yarn and draw end through last loop).

To bind off on the purl side:

Step 1: Purl the first 2 stitches. Now insert left needle into the first stitch on right needle, and pull it over the second stitch and completely off the needle. You have now bound off one stitch.

Step 2: Purl one more stitch; insert left needle into first stitch on right needle and pull it over the new stitch and completely off the needle. Another stitch is bound off.

Repeat Step 2 until all sts are bound off.

Yarn Over (YO)

To make a yarn over before a knit stitch, bring yarn to front of work as if you were going to purl, then take it over the right needle to the back into the position for knitting; then knit the next stitch (*Fig 41*).

To make a yarn over before a purl stitch, bring yarn around right needle from front to back, then back around into position for purling; purl the next stitch (*Fig 42*).

ABBREVIATIONS

beg . . . . begin(ning)
ch(s) . . . . chain(s)
dc . . . . double crochet(s)
dec . . . . decrease (-ing)
dpn . . . . double pointed needles
EOR . . . . every other row
fig . . . . figure
hdc . . . . half double crochet(s)
inc . . . . increase (-ing)
K . . . . knit
lp(s) . . . . loop(s)
P . . . . purl
patt . . . . pattern
prev . . . . previous
PSSO . . . . pass slip stitch over
rem . . . . remain(ing)
rep . . . . repeat(ing)
rnd(s) . . . . round(s)
sc . . . . single crochet(s)
sk . . . . skip
sl . . . . slip
sl st(s) . . . . slip stitch(es)
sp(s) . . . . space(s)
st(s) . . . . stitch(es)
stock st . . . . stockinette stitch, knit 1 row, purl 1 row
tch . . . . turning chain
tog . . . . together
tr(c) . . . . triple crochet(s)
YO . . . . yarn over

work even: This term in instructions means to continue working in the pattern as established, without increasing or decreasing.

SYMBOLS

*   An asterisk is used to mark the beginning of a portion of instructions which will be worked more than once; thus, "rep from * twice" means after working the instructions once, repeat the instructions following the asterisk twice more (3 times in all).

†   The dagger identifies a portion of instructions that will be repeated again later in the pattern.

=   The number after an equal sign at the end of a row/rnd indicates the number of stitches you should have when the row/rnd has been completed.

( )   Parentheses are used to enclose instructions which should be worked the exact number of times specified immediately following the parentheses, such as: (K1, P1) twice. They are also used to set off and clarify a group of sts that are to be worked all into the same sp or st, such as (D dc, ch 1, D dc) in corner sp.

[ ]   Brackets and ( ) parentheses are used to provide additional information to clarify instructions.

GAUGE

It is essential to achieve the gauge—number of stitches and rows per inch—given in patt in order to make the correct size.

Before beginning your project, refer to the Gauge Note and make a gauge swatch using the hook or needle and yarn specified. Work several rows; finish off. Place work on a flat surface and measure sts in center of piece. If you have more sts to the inch than specified, use a larger size hook or needle. If you have fewer sts to the inch than specified, use a smaller size hook or needle. Then make another gauge swatch and check your gauge once again. Do not hesitate to change hook size to obtain the specified gauge. Often you will not be able to achieve gauge with the size hook or needle recommended.

While working, continue to check your gauge. Select sts/rnds near the center of your work, using small safety pins or straight pins to identify the sts to be measured and always measure over two or more inches.

LITTLE TREE-TOP ANGEL

designed by Sue Penrod

For something a little different, here's a tree-top angel who looks a bit devilish with his halo only slightly tarnished. He's easy and fun to make if you follow these suggestions. (1) Be sure to check your gauge. If not worked to gauge, the angel will not be shaped properly. (2) Do not overstuff. Excess stuffing will change the shape of the entire doll.

Size
Approx 7″ tall (*without halo*)

Materials
Worsted weight yarn:
    2 oz white
    1½ oz gold
Size H aluminum crochet hook (*or size required for gauge*)
Plastic doll head with turned-up nose (*2½″ high, including neck*)
Plastic doll hands (*1½″ long, including wrist*)
12″ Chenille stem in white or gold (*for halo*)
Polyester fiber (*for stuffing*)

Gauge
In sc, 4 sts = 1″; 4 rnds = 1″

Instructions
NOTE: Throughout patt, unless otherwise specified, work continuous rnds without joining. Use a small safety pin or piece of yarn in contrasting color and mark first st of rnd; move marker at beg of each rnd.

BODY: Beg at neck edge, with white (leave approx 12″ end for securing head later), ch 9 loosely, join with a sl st to form a ring. (*NOTE: Before proceeding, check size of ring by slipping up over neck of doll head. If sts are too tight, start again and work chains looser. Remove head before continuing.*)

Rnd 1: Sc in each ch around (do not join) = 9 sc.

Rnd 2: Sc in each sc around.

Rnd 3: * Sc in each of next 2 sc, 2 sc in next sc; rep from * around = 12 sc.

Rnd 4: Rep Rnd 3 = 16 sc.

Rnd 5: * Sc in each of next 2 sc, 2 sc in next sc; rep from * to last sc, sc in last sc = 21 sc.

Rnd 6: Rep Rnd 3 = 28 sc.

Rnds 7 through 11: Rep Rnd 2, 5 times.

Rnd 12: * Sc in each of next 3 sc, 2 sc in next sc; rep from * around = 35 sc.

Rnds 13 through 20: Rep Rnd 2, 8 times.

Rnd 21 (bottom edging): Working **in front lp** (lp toward you) of each st around, work (sl st, ch 3) in next sc, dc in next sc; * 2 dc in next sc, dc in each of next 2 sc; rep from * around, join with a sl st in top of beg ch-3 = 46 dc (counting beg ch-3). Finish off; weave in ends. (*NOTE: Back lps will be used to work bottom closure of body.*)

Insert head into neck opening. Thread beg end into tapestry or yarn needle and weave through sts around neck edge twice. Draw up tightly to secure head; fasten end securely. Stuff and shape body; then work bottom closure.

BOTTOM CLOSURE: Hold angel with head toward you and bottom edging (last rnd worked) at top.

Rnd 1: Working **in unused lp** of each st behind edging, make a slip knot on hook with white, then join with a sc in any lp around; * sk next lp, sc in next lp; rep from * around, join with a sl st **in both lps** of beg sc = 18 sc. Continue by working **in both lps** of sts.

Rnd 2: Ch 2, * sk next sc, hdc in next sc; rep from * to last sc, sk last sc, join with a sl st in top of beg ch-2 = 9 hdc (counting beg ch-2). Before working next rnd, finish stuffing body.

Rnd 3: Ch 2, * sk next st, hdc in next st; rep from * around = 5 hdc. Finish off, leaving approx 6″ end. Thread into tapestry or yarn needle and weave through sts of last rnd. Draw up tightly and fasten securely.

ARMS AND SLEEVES (make 2): Beg at wrist end of arm, with white (leave approx 10″ end to secure hand later), ch 6 loosely, join with a sl st to form a ring.

(*NOTE: Check size of ring for slipping up over wrist end of hand.*)

Rnd 1: Sc in each ch around = 6 sc. Do not join; work continuous rnds (mark first st of rnd as before).

Rnd 2: Sc in each sc around.

Rnds 3 through 10: Rep Rnd 2, 8 times. At end of Rnd 10, do not finish off. Insert hand into beg opening of arm and secure in place in same manner as head. Lightly stuff arm to within last rnd from top. Pinch last rnd closed. Continuing with same yarn and working through **both sides** at the same time, sc in each of 3 corresponding sts across (opening closed). Do not finish off; continue with sleeve (working in rnds) as follows:

Rnd 11: (*NOTE: Sts of sleeve are worked on inside of rnd; wrong side of sts will now be facing outside of sleeve.*) Ch 1, turn; with wrong side of closure sts just worked facing you, word 2 sc **in back lp** in each of 3 sc (closure sts) across. Turn; work 2 sc **in unused lp** in each of 3 closure sts across (behind 6 sc just made) = 12 sc. Do not join; work continuous rnds (mark first st of rnd as before). Continue by working rnds on inside **in both lps** of sts.

Rnd 12: * Sc in next sc, 2 sc in next sc; rep from * around = 18 sc.

Rnds 13 through 22: Rep Rnd 2, 10 times. At end of Rnd 22, join with a sl st in beg sc. Finish off and weave in end. Turn sleeve down over arm (wrong side of sts will now be on inside of sleeve). Sew arm and sleeve unit to side of angel, approx 1″ down from neck.

HALO: With gold, ch 35.

Row 1: Sc in 2nd ch from hook and in each rem ch across = 34 sc.

Row 2: Ch 1, turn; sc in each sc across.

Row 3: Rep Row 2. Finish off, leaving approx 24″ sewing length; thread into tapestry or yarn needle. Having right side of sts facing stem, cover chenille stem to within 3″ of one end (leave 3″ uncovered for inserting into body later); sew edges tog. Bend approx 6½″ of covered end of stem into a circle to form halo; tack end in place. Insert uncovered end into body at center back (*Fig 1*), approx 2 rnds down from neck. Tack stem of halo to sts at neck to secure in place.

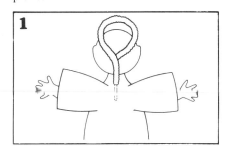

WINGS (worked in one piece): Beg at tip of one wing, with gold, ch 4, join with a sl st to form a ring. (*NOTE: Be careful to work all following rnds on right side.*)

Rnd 1: Sc in each ch around = 4 sc. Do not join; work continuous rnds (mark first st of rnd as before).

Rnd 2: * Sc in next sc, 2 sc in next sc; rep from * around = 6 sc.

Rnd 3: Rep Rnd 2 = 9 sc.

Rnd 4: * Sc in each of next 2 sc, 2 sc in next sc; rep from * around = 12 sc.

Rnd 5: Rep Rnd 4 = 16 sc.

Rnd 6: Rep Rnd 2 = 24 sc.

Rnd 7: Sc in each sc around.

Rnds 8 and 9: Rep Rnd 7, twice.

Rnd 10: * Sk next sc, sc in next sc; rep from * around = 12 sc.

Rnd 11: Rep Rnd 7. One wing is now completed; continue with other wing.

Rnd 12: Work 2 sc in each sc around = 24 sc.

Rnds 13 through 15: Rep Rnd 7, 3 times.

Rnd 16: * Sc in next sc, sk next sc, sc in next sc; rep from * around = 16 sc.

Rnd 17: * Sc in each of next 2 sc, sk next sc, sc in next sc; rep from * around = 12 sc.

Rnd 18: Rep Rnd 17 = 9 sc.

Rnds 19 and 20: Rep Rnd 16, twice. At end of Rnd 20, you should have 4 sc. Do not finish off; continue with bottom edging.

Bottom edging: Hold both thicknesses of wings tog and work edging across one long shaped edge of wings as follows: Work (ch 3, sc) in each rnd across to tip of other wing. Finish off; weave in ends.

With gold, sew center of wings through both thicknesses to center back of angel, just below stem of halo at neck.

MINI CHRISTMAS STOCKINGS

These little decorations are quick and easy to make, and add charm to tree or package. Add some candy canes, holly or small poinsettia sprigs and you have a perfect small gift.

KNITTED SANTA SOCK TREE DECORATION

designed by Judy Demain

Size

Approx 2″ wide (*across top*) × 4″ long (*from top edge to base of heel*).

Materials

Worsted weight yarn:
    15 yds red
    4 yds white
Size 6, 10″ straight knitting needles (*or size required for gauge*)

Gauge

In stock st, 5 sts = 1″; 7 rows = 1″

Instructions

Beg at top, with white, cast on 20 sts. Knit 6 rows even for garter st cuff. Cut white, leaving approx 16″ sewing length for cuff seam and loop; join red, leaving approx 20″ end for sewing back and sole seam later. Change to stock st (knit 1 row, purl 1 row) and work even for 16 more rows, ending by working a purl row. Now work instep.

INSTEP: Row 1 (dividing row): K 13 (leave rem 7 sts unworked).

Row 2: P6 (leave rem 7 sts unworked). Continuing on center 6 sts only, work 4 more rows even in stock st, ending by working a purl row. Cut yarn, leaving sts on needle. Continue with foot shaping.

FOOT: With right side facing you and using right-hand needle (with 7 sts at right-hand edge on it), join red and pick up 6 sts along right edge of instep, then knit across 6 instep sts, pick up 6 sts along left edge of instep, knit rem 7 sts = 32 sts now on one needle.

Row 2: Purl.

Row 3: K2 tog; * K 13, K2 tog; rep from * once more = 29 sts.

Row 4: Purl.

115

Row 5: K2 tog, * K 11, K2 tog; K 12, K2 tog = 26 sts.

Row 6: Purl.

Row 7: K2 tog; * K 10, K2 tog; rep from * once more = 23 sts.

Row 8: Purl. Bind off all sts in knit.

Finish off red. Thread 20″ red sewing length (below cuff) into tapestry or yarn needle and sew back and sole seam. Then thread 16″ white sewing length (at base of cuff) into tapestry or yarn needle and sew seam on cuff. Do not finish off; make 1″ yarn loop at top of stocking and then fasten end securely. Weave in ends.

CROCHETED ICE SKATE DECORATION

adapted from a design by Sue Penrod

Size

Approx 1½″ wide (*across top*) × 2½″ long (*from top edge to bottom of blade*).

Materials

Worsted weight yarn:
    10 yds white
    2½ yds red
    2 yds grey

Size I aluminum crochet hook (*or size required for gauge*)

Gauge

In sc, 7 sts = 2″

Instructions

Beg at top, with white (leave approx 12″ end for working loop later), ch 10, join with a sl st to form a ring. (*NOTE: All rnds are worked on outside of skate.*)

Rnd 1: Sc in each ch around = 10 sc. *NOTE: Do not join; work continuous rnds. Use a small safety pin or piece of yarn in contrasting color and mark first st of rnd; move marker at beg of each rnd.*

Rnds 2 through 4: Sc in each sc around for 3 rnds.

Rnd 5: Sc in next sc, dec over next 2 sc (**To work Dec: Draw up a lp in each next 2 sc, YO hook and draw through all 3 lps on hook = dec made**). Sc in each of next 2 sc, 2 sc in each of next 4 sc, sc in next sc = 13 sc.

Rnd 6: Sc in each of next 6 sc, 2 sc in next sc; work (sc, hdc) in next sc, work (hdc, sc) in next sc; 2 sc in next sc, sc in each of next 3 sc = 17 sts.

Rnd 7: Sc in each of next 9 sc, 2 sc in each of next 2 hdc, sc in each of next 6 sc = 19 sc.

Rnd 8: Sc in each of 19 sc around, sc in next sc (first st of rnd), sl st in next sc. Finish off white.

BLADE: Join grey with sl st in 2nd st of rnd (where last sl st was just worked). Pinch opening closed. **Working through both sides at the same time**, work (hdc, sc) in next st, sc in each of next 7 sts, work (hdc, ch 2, sl st) in last st. Finish off; weave in ends.

LOOP: Insert hook in st at top edge under beg yarn end, hook yarn end and draw through st; ch 10, join with a sl st in same st. Finish off; weave in end securely.

LACE: Thread 18″ strand of red into tapestry or yarn needle. Beg at center top of skate and work 3 cross sts evenly spaced down center front of skate (**Fig 1**). Tie ends of lace into a bow and trim ends evenly.

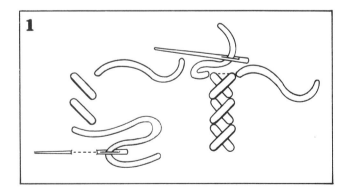

1

POMPON: Make a ½″ diameter red pompon as follows: Wrap yarn around tines of dinner fork; then tie wrapped yarn securely between the center of the tines. Cut looped ends and trim to ½″ diameter size. Attach pompon securely to toe end of skate.

CROCHETED SNOWFLAKES

designed by Mary Thomas

Lacy snowflakes are pretty to hang in a window, a doorway, or on a tree. They work up quickly, and will make treasured gifts.

Sizes

Snowflake No. 1, approx 3½″ across from side to side.
Snowflake No. 2, approx 6″ across from point to point.

Materials

Bedspread-weight crochet cotton in white:
    12 yds for Snowflake No. 1, or
    20 yds for Snowflake No. 2
Size 5 steel crochet hook (*or size required for gauge*)

Gauge

In dc, 8 sts = 1″

SNOWFLAKE NO. 1

Instructions

Ch 8, join with a sl st to form a ring.

Rnd 1: Ch 4, work 23 trc in ring, join with a sl st in top of beg ch-4.

Rnd 2: Ch 3, do not turn; dc in same st as joining, * † ch 6, sl st in 5th ch from hook (for picot) †; rep from † to † twice (3 picots now made), ch 1, sk next 3 trc, work 2 dc in next trc; rep from * 4 times more, then rep from † to † 3 times (for last picot lp); ch 1, sk last 3 trc, join with a sl st in top of beg ch-3 = 6 picot lps.

Rnd 3: Ch 4, do not turn; trc in next dc, * † ch 6, sl st in 5th ch from hook (for picot) †; rep from † to † 4 times (5 picots now made), ch 1, trc in each of next 2 dc (between picot lps); rep from * 4 times more, then rep from † to † 5 times; ch 1, join with a sl st in top of beg ch-4. **Do not finish off**; continue with same thread and work hanger.

HANGER: Ch 20, do not turn; sl st in next trc, finish off. Weave in ends securely.

Finishing

Wash, block and starch, following directions on page 109.

SNOWFLAKE NO. 2

Instructions

Ch 6, join with a sl st to form a ring.

Rnd 1: Ch 1, work 12 sc in ring, join with a sl st in beg sc.

Rnd 2: Do not turn; * ch 16, sl st in next sc; rep from * 10 times more, ch 7, work a triple trc in sl st (st used to join prev rnd). [**To work triple trc: (YO hook) 4 times, insert hook in sl st and draw up a lp (6 lps now on hook), work (YO hook and draw through 2 lps on hook) 5 times = triple trc made**] = 12 lps. (*NOTE: Last lp was formed by working ch 7 and triple trc, and brings thread into position to beg next rnd.*)

Rnd 3: Do not turn; * ch 6, sc over center of next lp; rep from * 10 times more, ch 3, sk ch-7 of last lp, dc in top of triple trc of same lp = 12 lps. (*NOTE: Last lp was formed by working ch 3 and dc, and brings thread into position to beg next rnd.*)

Rnd 4: Ch 6, do not turn; work 3 dc in first lp (over last dc of prev rnd), * work (3 dc, ch 3, 3 dc) in next lp; rep from * 10 times more, work 2 dc in first lp (next to ch-6 and first 3 dc of rnd), join with a sl st in 3rd ch of beg ch-6.

Rnd 5: Do not turn; sl st into next ch-3 sp, ch 5, work a double trc in same sp. [**To work double trc: (YO hook) 3 times, insert hook in sp and draw up a lp (5 lps now on hook), work (YO hook and draw through 2 lps on hook) 4 times = double trc made**] * Ch 5, 2 double trc in same sp; ch 11 (for lp at point), 2 double trc in same sp; ch 5, 2 double trc in same sp; ch 5, sk next two 3-dc groups, sc in next ch-3 sp; ch 5, sk next two 3-dc groups, 2 double trc in next ch-3 sp; rep from * around, ending last rep without working last 2 double trc, join with a sl st in top of beg ch-5. Finish off and weave in ends.

Finishing

Starch and block snowflake same as for Snowflake No. 1. For hanger, use a piece of white or translucent nylon thread (or fishing line) to tie a loop at one point of snowflake.

CROCHETED PINEAPPLE ORNAMENT

For a tree decoration or package tie-on, what could be prettier than this double-sided pineapple design? Make them in green, red, gold, or white for a really festive look.

Size
Approx 5″ wide × 5″ long

Materials
Bedspread-weight crochet cotton
    90 yds bright green
Size 7 steel crochet hook (*or size required for gauge*)
3″ plastic foam egg
1 yd gold cord

Gauge
One shell (2 dc, ch 3, 2 dc) = ½″

Instructions

(Make 2) Ch 6, join with a sl st to form a ring.

Row 1 (right side): Ch 3, work (dc, ch 3, 2 dc) in ring; ch 8, work (2 dc, ch 3, 2 dc) in ring.

Row 2: Ch 5, turn; work (2 dc, ch 3, 2 dc) in first ch-3 sp (shell made); ch 4, work 15 sc in next ch-8 sp (for base of pineapple); ch 4, work a shell in next ch-3 sp.

Row 3: Ch 5, turn; shell in sp of first shell, ch 4, sk next ch-4 sp, dc in first sc of pineapple, (ch 1, sk next sc, dc in next sc of pineapple) 7 times; ch 4, sk next ch-4 sp, shell in sp of next shell.

Row 4: Ch 5, turn; shell in sp of first shell, ch 4, sk next ch-4 sp, sc in first dc of pineapple, (sc in next ch-1 sp and in next dc of pineapple) 7 times; ch 4, sk next ch-4 sp, shell in sp of next shell.

Row 5: Ch 5, turn; shell in sp of first shell, ch 4, sk next ch-4 sp, dc in first sc of pineapple, (ch 1, dc in next sc of pineapple) 14 times; ch 4, sk next ch-4 sp, shell in sp of next shell.

Row 6: Ch 5, turn; shell in sp of first shell, ch 4, sk next ch-4 sp, sc in first dc of pineapple, (sc in next ch 1 sp and next dc of pineapple) 14 times; ch 4, sk next ch-4 sp, shell in sp of next shell.

Row 7: Ch 5, turn; shell in sp of first shell, ch 4, sk next ch-4 sp, sc in first sc of pineapple, (ch 4, sk next sc, sc in next sc of pineapple) 14 times; ch 4, sk next ch-4 sp, shell in sp of next shell.

Row 8: Ch 5, turn; shell in sp of first shell, ch 4, sk next ch-4 sp, sc in first sp of pineapple, (ch 4, sc in next sp of pineapple) 13 times; ch 4, sk next ch-4 sp, shell in sp of next shell.

Rows 9 through 20: Rep Row 8, 12 times, having one ch-4 sp less on pineapple on each row. (*NOTE: At end of Row 20, you should have one sp rem on top of pineapple.*)

Row 21: Ch 5, turn; shell in sp of first shell, ch 4, sc in last sp of pineapple; ch 4, sk next ch-4 sp, 2 dc in sp of next shell; ch 1, sl st back into sp of first shell (shells now joined); ch 1, 2 dc in sp of 2nd shell (where last 2 dc were just worked).

Row 22: Ch 5, turn; sl st in sl st between shells (st joining shells tog). Finish off; weave in ends.

Finishing

Block pieces out to size. Next place styrofoam egg between crocheted pieces, having right side of each piece facing outward and edges carefully matched. Beg at center top sp and weave cord through corresponding ch-4 sps (between pineapple design and outer shells) around ornament, ending in center top sp. Pull up cord tightly and tie into a knot; do not cut. Leave approx 3″ of cord free above ornament (for loop to hang ornament to tree), knot strands tog and then tie cord into a small bow. Trim ends evenly.

CROCHETED CHRISTMAS TABLE TREE

designed by Mary Thomas

Decorate your home for the holidays with this lovely crocheted tree ideal for a table centerpiece. If you wish, you can use purchased pompons or small ornaments in place of yarn pompons.

Size

Approx 13½″ tall (*including pompon on top*)

Materials

Worsted weight yarn:
    11 oz ombre in shades of green
    1 oz bright red (*for pompons*)
    5 yds bright yellow (*for pompon at top of tree*)
Size J aluminum crochet hook (*or size required for gauge*)
Polyester fiber (*for stuffing*)

Gauge

In sc, 13 sts = 4″; 4 rows = 1″

Instructions

(**Make 6**) Beg at bottom edge, with ombre, ch 57.
Row 1: Sc in 2nd ch from hook, sk next ch, sc in each of next 7 chs; hdc in each of next 5 chs, dc in each of next 28 chs; hdc in each of next 5 chs, sc in each of next 7 chs; sk next ch, sc in last ch = 54 sts.

Row 2: Ch 1, turn; sk first sc, dec over next 2 sc [**To work dec: Draw up a lp in each of next 2 sc (3 lps now on hook), YO hook and draw through all 3 lps on hook = dec made**]. Sc in each rem st across to last 3 sc, sk next sc, dec over last 2 sc = 50 sc.

Row 3: Ch 1, turn; sk first sc, sc in each of next 17 sc, hdc in each of next 14 sc; sc in each of next 16 sc, sk next sc, sc in last sc = 48 sts.

Row 4: Ch 1, turn; sk first sc, sc in each rem st across to last 2 sc; sk next sc, sc in last sc = 46 sc.

Rows 5 through 12: Rep Row 4, 8 times. (*NOTE: At end of Row 12, you should have 30 sc.*)

Row 13: Ch 9 (for branch), turn; sc in 2nd ch from hook, sk next ch, sc in each of rem 6 chs; sc in each rem sc across = 37 sc.

Row 14: Ch 9 (for branch), turn; sc in 2nd ch from hook, sk next ch, sc in each of rem 6 chs; sc in each rem sc across to last 3 sc, sk next sc, dec over last 2 sc = 42 sc.

Row 15: Ch 1, turn; sk first sc, sc in each rem sc across to last 3 sc; sk next sc, dec over last 2 sc = 39 sc.

Rows 16 through 26: Rep Row 4, 11 times. (*NOTE: At end of Row 26, you should have 17 sc.*)

Row 27: Ch 9 (for branch), turn; sc in 2nd ch from hook, sk next ch, sc in each of rem 6 chs; sc in each rem sc across to last 2 sc, sk next sc, sc in last sc = 23 sc.

Row 28: Rep Row 14 = 28 sc.

Row 29: Rep Row 15 = 25 sc.

Rows 30 through 34: Rep Row 4, 5 times. (*NOTE: At end of Row 34, you should have 15 sc.*)

Row 35: Ch 1, turn; sc in each sc across.

Ros 36: Rep Row 4 = 13 sc.

Rows 37 through 46: Rep Rows 35 and 36, 5 times. (*NOTE: At end of Row 46, you should have 3 sc.*)

Row 47: Ch 1, turn; sc in each sc across.

Row 48: Ch 1, turn; sk first sc, dec over last 2 sc. Finish off; weave in ends.

Assembling

Join two pieces tog to form one section of tree as follows: Hold both pieces tog with edges carefully matched. Leaving approx 7″ open at center bottom for stuffing later, beg at bottom and sc edges tog around with ombre—be sure to work through matching sts/rows around and to work 3 sc at tip of each branch and at center top. Finish off, leaving approx 16″ sewing length. Stuff tip of each branch lightly (do not overstuff). Join rem pieces tog in same manner to form other two sections of tree and lightly stuff tip of each branch.

Place all 3 sections of tree just made on top of each other, having edges in same alignment. Thread approx 48″

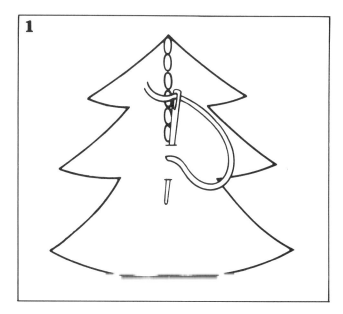

strand of ombre into a tapestry or yarn needle. Using the backstitch sewing method, beg at top and sew all 3 sections tog down the center (***Fig 1***), ending at bottom edge. Finish stuffing and shaping sections, then sew bottom openings closed.

POMPONS: Make 12, 1″ diameter red pompons (see Pompon instructions on page 28), leaving tying ends of each pompon uncut. Using these yarn ends, attach one pompon under tip of each of the 12 upper branches around tree and tie ends into a small bow. Then make one, 1″ diameter yellow pompon and attach securely to top of tree.

JINGLE TREE CHRISTMAS DECORATION

designed by Mary Thomas

Ten small wreaths are joined to form this very joyful and festive decoration. Or perhaps, you may wish to make only one wreath and use it for a tree ornament, package decoration, or as a lapel pin.

Size

Approx 12″ wide × 15″ long

Materials

Worsted weight yarn:
    1½ oz forest green
    5 yds bright red
Size G aluminum crochet hook (*or size required for gauge*)
Ten 2″ diameter metal macrame rings or 1¾″ plastic rings (*from sealed caps on plastic gallon milk containers*)
One 1″ diameter plastic ring (*for top ring*)
Ten 13 mm diameter gold jingle bells

(*MATERIALS NOTE: Yarn amount needed to make one wreath is 7 yds green and ½ yd red.*)

Gauge

One wreath = 3″ diameter

Instructions

WREATH (make 10): With green (*leave approx 8″ end for attaching jingle bell later*), make a slip knot on hook.

Rnd 1: Work 30 sc over larger size ring, join with a sl st in beg sc.

Rnd 2: * Ch 3, sl st in next sc; rep from * around, ch 3, join with a sl st in joining sl st of prev rnd. Finish off.

Slip jingle bell onto 8″ end (*left at beg of wreath*) and position at center of wreath. Tie yarn into a knot at top of bell; then weave yarn end into wreath, directly above bell (*you should now have a double strand holding bell*).

For bow, thread 18″ length of red into tapestry or yarn needle. With right side of sts on wreath facing you, beg in ch-3 sp directly above bell and weave yarn through ch-3 sps around wreath. Tie ends into a small bow and trim.

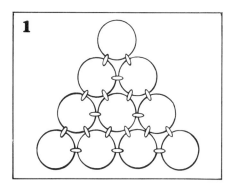

1

Assembling

Position wreaths as shown in **Fig 1**, having right side of each wreath facing up. Tack wreaths tog as indicated.

TOP RING: With green, make a slip knot on hook, then work 16 scs over 1″ diameter ring, join with a sl st in beg sc. Finish off, leaving approx 6″ sewing length. Tack ring securely to top wreath of tree.

TREE TRUNK: With green (*leave approx 12″ sewing length*), ch 7.

Row 1 (right side): Sc in 2nd ch from hook and in each rem ch across = 6 sc.

Row 2: Ch 1, turn; sc in each sc across.

Rows 3 through 9: Rep Row 2, 7 times. At end of Row 9, finish off and weave in this end. Tack each end of foundation chain edge to center two bottom wreaths of tree.

CHRISTMAS STOCKINGS

CROCHETED MARY JANE CHRISTMAS SOCK

designed by Carol Wilson Mansfield and Mary Thomas

Delight a little girl on Christmas morning with this charming Mary Jane shoe complete with white sock decorated with red and green ruffles. It's cute enough to hang on her wall all year. Made in easy single crochet.

Size

Approx 6¼" wide (*across top of cuff*) × 9" long (*from folded edge of cuff to base of heel*).

Materials

Worsted weight yarn:
    2½ oz white
    ½ oz black
    8 yds red
    8 yds light green
Size H aluminum crochet hook (*or size required for gauge*)
White button (⅝ *diameter*)

Gauge

In sc, 11 sts = 3"; 4 rows = 1"

Instructions

Beg at top, with white, ch 45.

Row 1 (right side): Sc in 2nd ch from hook and in each rem ch across = 44 sc.

Rows 2 through 12: Work 11 rows even. (*NOTE: To "work even" on each row, ch 1, turn; sc in each sc across.*)

Row 13: Ch 1, turn; sc in each of first 11 sc, * dec over next 2 sc. (**To make dec: Draw up a lp in each of next 2 sc, YO hook and draw through all 3 lps on hook = dec made**); sc in each of next 9 sc; rep from * twice more = 41 sc.

Rows 14 through 18: Work 5 rows even.

Row 19: Ch 1, turn; sc in each of first 10 sc, dec over next 2 sc; sc in each of next 17 sc, dec over next 2 sc; sc in each of rem 10 sc = 39 sc.

Rows 20 through 24: Work 5 rows even.

Row 25: Ch 1, turn; sc in each of first 9 sc, * dec over next 2 sc, sc in each of next 8 sc; rep from * twice more = 36 sc.

Rows 26 through 30: Work 5 rows even. At end of Row 30, finish off white, leaving approx 24″ sewing length for sewing back seam later.

INSTEP: Hold work with last row just worked at top and 24″ sewing length at upper right-hand corner.

Row 1: Sk first 6 sc, join white with a sl st in next sc; ch 1, sc in each of next 23 sc (leave rem 6 sc unworked).

Row 2: Ch 1, turn; sk first sc, sc in each rem sc across = 22 sc.

Rows 3 through 10: Rep Row 2, 8 times. (*NOTE: You will be decreasing one sc in each row—at end of Row 9, you should have 14 sc.*) Finish off white; join black.

Rows 11 and 12: With black, work 2 rows even.

Rows 13 through 16: Rep Row 2, 4 times. (*NOTE: At end of Row 16, you should have 10 sc.*) Finish off black.

FOOT: Hold work with instep just worked at top and 24″ white sewing length at right-hand edge. Join black (leave approx 12″ end for sewing heel seam later) with a sl st in first sc at right-hand edge (next to 24″ sewing length).

Row 1: Ch 1, sc in same st as joining; 2 sc in next sc, sc in each of next 4 sc, 2 sc in next sc at inside corner. **Continuing across right edge of instep**, 2 sc in first row, sc in each of next 9 white rows, sc in each of next 5 black rows (leave last black row unworked). **Continuing across toe edge**, dec over first 2 sc, sc in each of next 6 sc, dec over last 2 sc. **Continuing across left edge of instep**, sc in each of next 5 black rows, sc in each of next 9 white rows; 2 sc in next row and in next sc at inside corner. Sc in each of next 4 sc, 2 sc in next sc, sc in last sc = 58 sc.

Row 2: Ch 1, turn; sc in each sc across.

Row 3: Ch 1, turn; sc in each of first 25 sc, dec over next 2 sc, sc in each of next 4 sc, dec over next 2 sc; sc in each of rem 25 sc = 56 sc.

Row 4: Rep Row 2.

Row 5: Ch 1, turn; sc in each of first 25 sc, (dec over next 2 sc) 3 times; sc in each of rem 25 sc = 53 sc.

Row 6: Rep Row 2.

Row 7: Ch 1, turn; sc in first sc, dec over next 2 sc, sc in each of next 23 sc; dec over next 2 sc, sc in each of next 22 sc; dec over next 2 sc, sc in last sc = 50 sc.

Row 8: Ch 1, turn; sc in each of first 23 sc, (dec over next 2 sc) twice; sc in each of rem 23 sc = 48 sc. Finish off black, leaving approx 18″ sewing length.

Finishing

With matching yarn and overcast st, sew bottom, heel and back seam.

STRAP: With black (leave approx 6″ end for sewing strap to stocking later), ch 3.

Row 1: Sc in 2nd ch from hook and in next ch = 2 sc.

Row 2: Ch 1, turn; sc in each sc across.
Rep Row 2 until strap measures approx 7″ long. Finish off, leaving approx 6″ sewing length. Sew each end of strap to top edge of shoe (on each side of ankle), having one end of strap overlapping approx ½″ of shoe. Sew button to overlapped end of strap.

CUFF: Working on inside of stocking, join white with a sl st at top edge at seam.

Rnd 1: Ch 15 (for loop), sl st in same sp as joining; sc in each of 44 sts around. (*NOTE: Do not join; work continuous rnds. Use a small safety pin or piece of yarn in contrasting color and mark first st of rnd; move marker at beg of each rnd.*)

Rnd 2: Hold loop down in front of work, * 2 sc in next sc, sc in each of next 10 sc; rep from * 3 times more = 48 sc.

Rnds 3 through 5: Work 3 rnds even. (*NOTE: To "work even," sc in each sc around for specified number of rnds, without increasing or decreasing.*) At end of Rnd 5, drop white (do not cut—will be used again later); join red (for ruffle).

Rnd 6 (ruffle): With red, * sl st **in front lp** (lp toward you—back lp will be used in next rnd) of next sc, ch 3; rep from * around. Finish off red.

Rnd 7: With white, sc **in unused lp** (back lp) of each sc around (behind ruffle) = 48 sc.

Rnd 8: Sc **in both lps** of each sc around. Finish off white; join green (for ruffle).

Rnd 9: With green, * sl st **in both lps** of next sc, ch 3; rep from * around, join with a sl st in first ch of beg ch-3. Finish off; weave in all ends. Fold down cuff.

KNITTED GIANT ARGYLE CHRISTMAS STOCKING

designed by Carol Wilson Mansfield and Mary Thomas

Remember when you used to knit argyles for your favorite BMOC (Big Man On Campus)? Here's a giant size version that's sure to bring back happy memories. In case it's been a long time since you've knitted with bobbins, or you've never made an argyle before, we've included complete instructions.

Size

Approx 7½" wide (*across top*) × 15" long (*from top edge to base of heel*).

Materials

Worsted weight yarn:
    4 oz bright green
    ¾ oz bright red
    ½ oz white
    10 yds bright blue
Size 8, 10" straight knitting needles (*or size required for gauge*)
Size 8, 7" double pointed needles (*abbreviated dpn*)— or size required for gauge
21 yarn bobbins
2 stitch markers

Gauge

In stock sc, 9 sts = 2"; 6 rows/rnds = 1"

Techniques for Working Argyle Design

The design is worked in stock st from the chart in *Fig 1*, making color changes as indicated. Colors are repre-

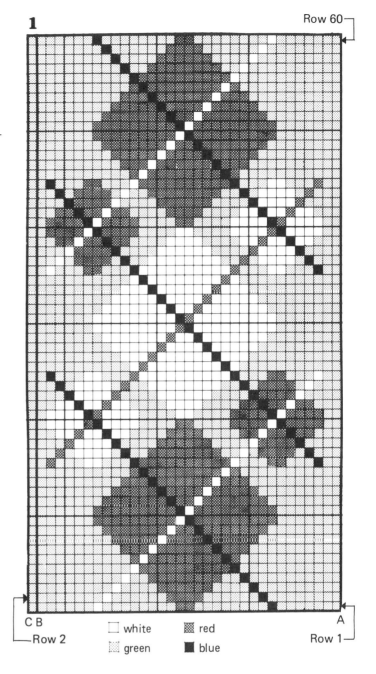

1 Row 60

C B ☐ white ▧ red
Row 2 ▨ green ■ blue A Row 1

sented on the chart by different symbols with the key for these symbols printed next to the chart. Each square on the chart represents one st and each horizontal row of squares represents one row of knitting. The chart is worked from the bottom to the top. The first and all odd-numbered rows are knitted across from A to B once; then from A to C once. The 2nd and all even-numbered rows are purled across from C to A once; then from B to A once.

A bobbin is used for each block of color. Use a separate bobbin for each diamond, each diagonal line, and each block of main color (between diamonds and on each end of row). Do not carry colors not in use across back of work, except across diagonal lines. When a bobbin is used for the first time, it is "tied in" to the color preceding

127

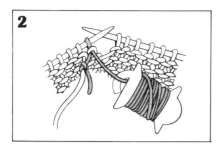

it (**Fig 2**). Later, when the stocking is finished, untie the knots before weaving in the yarn ends.

Color changes require the technique of crossing (twisting) the colors so no gap or hole appears in the stocking. To do this, bring the color you have just used in front and over to the left of the color you are going to use, bringing the new color up from underneath (**Fig 3**).

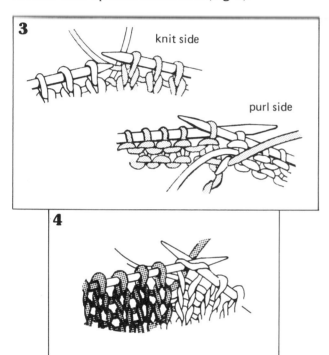

knit side

purl side

When the design slants diagonally to the right, the colors are crossed on the knit rows (**Fig 4**). On the purl rows, the colors will cross automatically as the purl st of the color being used encroaches into the color you are going to use next.

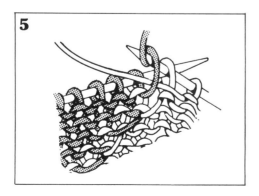

When the design slants diagonally to the left, the colors are crossed on the purl rows (**Fig 5**). On the knit rows, the colors will cross automatically as the knit st of the color being used encroaches into the color you are going to use next.

When the design is vertical, it is necessary to cross the colors on each row.

Instructions

Beg at top, with straight needles and green, cast on 67 sts.

Ribbing Row 1 (right side): * K1, P1; rep from * to last st, K1.

Ribbing Row 2: P1, * K1, P1; rep from * across. Rep Ribbing Rows 1 and 2, 4 times more. (*NOTE: You should now have a total of 10 rows of ribbing.*)

ARGYLE DESIGN: First, wind 9 bobbins as follows: 3 green, 2 red, 2 blue and 2 white. Begin design as follows: **Row 1 of Chart:** With first green bobbin, K7; tie in first blue bobbin, K1; continue with first green bobbin (bring yarn loosely across back of work) and K8; tie in first red bobbin, K2; tie in 2nd green bobbin, K8; tie in first white bobbin, K1; continue with 2nd green bobbin and K 13; tie in 2nd blue bobbin, K1; continue with 2nd green bobbin and K8; tie in 2nd red bobbin, K2; tie in 3rd green bobbin, K8; tie in 2nd white bobbin, K1; continue with 3rd green bobbin and K7. (First row of chart is now completed.) Now beg with **Row 2 of chart** and work through Row 60, making color changes as necessary. When all 60 rows of chart have been completed, change to dpns and work heel shaping and foot.

DIVIDE FOR HEEL: Continue with green only. **With first needle,** K 16 (first half of heel); **with 2nd needle,** K 17; **with 3rd needle,** K 18; sl rem 16 sts (other half of heel) onto first needle (you should now have a total of 32 sts on this needle). Do not finish off; continue with heel.

HEEL: Work back and forth in rows on 32 sts of heel.

Row 1 (right side): * K1, sl 1 as to purl; rep from * across.

Row 2: Purl. Rep last 2 rows until heel measures approx 2½" long, ending by working Row 1. Do not finish off; continue by turning heel.

TURN HEEL: (*NOTE: Heel is turned by working short rows; when instructions say "turn," leave rem sts unworked, turn work and begin next row.*)

Row 1 (wrong side): P 21; P2 tog, P1, turn.

Row 2: Sl 1 as to purl, K 11; sl 1 as to knit, K1, PSSO; K1, turn.

Row 3: Sl 1 as to purl, P 12; P2 tog, P1, turn.

Row 4: Sl 1 as to purl, K 13; sl 1 as to knit, K1, PSSO; K1, turn.

Row 5: Sl 1 as to purl, P 14; P2 tog, P1, turn.

Row 6: Sl 1 as to purl, K 15; sl 1 as to knit, K1, PSSO; K1, turn.

Row 7: Sl 1 as to purl, P 16; P2 tog, P1, turn.

Row 8: Sl 1 as to purl, K 17; sl 1 as to knit, K1, PSSO; K1, turn.

Row 9: Sl 1 as to purl, P 18; P2 tog, P1, turn.

Row 10: Sl 1 as to purl, K 19; sl 1 as to knit, K1, PSSO; K1 = 22 sts. Do not finish off; continue by working gusset and foot.

GUSSET AND FOOT: Rnd 1: Using needle with 22 heel sts, pick up 11 sts along right edge of heel, place marker, K6 from next needle. With free needle, K 12, then K 11 from next needle. With free needle, K6, place marker, pick up 11 sts along left edge of heel, K 11 from first needle (heel sts). (*NOTE: You should now have 79 sts total which are divided on 3 needles as follows: 28-23-28.*) Join and continue shaping in rnds.

Rnd 2: Knit to within 3 sts of first marker, K2 tog, K1; sl marker, knit to 2nd marker; sl marker, K1; sl 1 as to knit, K1, PSSO; knit rem sts = 77 sts. (*NOTE: Sl markers on each following rnd.*)

Rnd 3: Knit. Rep Rnds 2 and 3, 5 times more = 67 sts (22-23-22). Knit even until foot measures approx 6½″ from side edge of heel (where sts were picked up). Do not finish off; continue with toe shaping.

TOE: Rnd 1: * Knit to within 3 sts of marker, K2 tog, K1, sl marker; K1, sl 1 as to knit, K1, PSSO; rep from * once more, knit rem sts = 63 sts. Rep prev rnd, 12 times more = 15 sts.

Cut yarn, leaving approx 12″ end. Thread into tapestry or yarn needle and weave through rem sts twice (removing knitting needles). Draw up tightly and fasten securely.

Finishing

Weave in all ends. Lightly steam press argyle design on wrong side. Sew back seam. With straight needles and green, cast on 3 sts for loop. Knit even in rows for 5″. Bind off all sts, leaving approx 8″ sewing length. Fold in half and sew ends securely to top edge of stocking at back seam.

CROCHETED HIKING BOOT CHRISTMAS STOCKING

designed by Carol Wilson Mansfield and Mary Thomas

This hiking book with a real shoe lace is a great gift for the outdoors person in your life. It's made in easy single crochet.

Size

Approx 7″ wide (*across top of cuff*) × 11″ long (*from folded edge of cuff to base of heel*).

Materials

Rug yarn in 70-yd skeins:
    2¼ skeins rust
    ½ skein steel grey
    6 yds black
    4 yds grass green
    4 yds red
Size H aluminum crochet hook (*or size required for gauge*)
Ten ½″ gold metal D-rings
54″ red sport lace

Gauge

In sc, 7 sts = 2″; 7 rows = 2″

Instructions

Beg at top, with rust (leave approx 30″ end for sewing back seam later), ch 45.

Row 1 (right side): Sc in 2nd ch from hook and in each rem ch across = 44 sc.

Rows 2 through 8: Work 7 rows even. (*NOTE: To "work even" on each row, ch 1, turn; sc in each sc across.*)

Row 9 (marking row): Ch 1, turn; sc in each of first 16 sc, sc in next sc and mark this st for attaching D-ring later (use small safety pin or piece of yarn in contrasting color for marker); sc in each of next 10 sc, sc in next sc and mark this st (for attaching D-ring later); sc in each of rem 16 sc.

Rows 10 through 12: Work 3 rows even.

Row 13: Ch 1, turn; sc in each of first 11 sc, dec over next 2 sc. (**To make dec: Draw up a lp in each of next 2 sc, YO hook and draw through all 3 lps on hook = dec made**); sc in each of next 18 sc, dec over next 2 sc; sc in each of rem 11 sc = 42 sc.

Rows 14 through 16: Work 3 rows even.

Row 17 (marking row): Ch 1, turn; sc in each of first 15 sc, sc in next sc and mark this st; sc in each of next 10 sc, sc in next sc and mark this st; sc in each of rem 15 sc.

Row 18: Work even.

Row 19: Ch 1, turn; sc in each of first 10 sc, dec over next 2 sc; sc in each of next 18 sc, dec over next 2 sc; sc in each of rem 10 sc = 40 sc.

Rows 20 through 24: Work 5 rows even.

Row 25 (marking row): Ch 1, turn; sc in each of first 4 sc, dec over next 2 sc; sc in each of next 5 sc, dec over next 2 sc; sc in next sc, sc in next sc and mark this st; sc in each of next 10 sc, sc in next sc and mark this st; sc in next sc, dec over next 2 sc; sc in each of next 5 sc, dec over next 2 sc; sc in each of rem 4 sc = 36 sc.

Rows 26 through 30: Work 5 rows even. At end of Row 30, finish off rust.

INSTEP: Hold work with right side facing you (side with markers) and last row just worked at top.

Row 1: Sk first 6 sc, join rust with a sl st in next sc; ch 1, sc in each of next 23 sc (leave rem 6 sc unworked).

Row 2: Ch 1, turn; sk first sc, sc in each rem sc across = 22 sc.

Row 3 (marking row): Ch 1, turn; sk first sc, sc in each of next 4 sc; sc in next sc and mark this st, sc in each of next 10 sc; sc in next sc and mark this st, sc in each of rem 5 sc = 21 sc.

Rows 4 through 10: Rep Row 2, 7 times. (*NOTE: You will be decreasing one sc in each row—at end of Row 10, you should have 14 sc.*)

Row 11 (marking row): Ch 1, turn; sc in first sc, sc in next sc and mark this st; sc in each of next 10 sc, sc in next sc and mark this st; sc in last sc = 14 sc.

Row 12: Work even.

Rows 13 through 16: Rep Row 2, 4 times. (*NOTE: At end of Row 16, you should have 10 sc.*) Finish off rust.

FOOT: Hold work with right side facing you and instep just worked at top. Join rust with a sl st in first sc at right outer edge.

Row 1 (right side): Ch 1, sc in same st as joining; 2 sc in next sc, sc in each of next 4 sc, 2 sc in next sc at inside corner.

Continuing **across right edge of instep**, work 2 sc in first row, sc in each of next 14 rows (leave last row unworked).

Continuing **across toe edge**, dec over first 2 sc, sc in each of next 6 sc, dec over last 2 sc. Continuing **across left edge** of instep, sc in each of next 14 rows, work 2 sc in next row and in next sc at inside corner. Sc in each of next 4 sc, 2 sc in next sc, sc in last sc = 58 sc.

Row 2: Ch 1, turn; sc in each sc across.

Row 3: Ch 1, turn; sc in each of first 25 sc, dec over next 2 sc; sc in each of next 4 sc, dec over next 2 sc; sc in each of rem 25 sc = 56 sc.

Row 4: Rep Row 2.

Row 5: Ch 1, turn; sc in each of first 25 sc, (dec over next 2 sc) 3 times; sc in each of rem 25 sc = 53 sc.

Row 6: Rep Row 2.

Row 7: Ch 1, turn; sc in first sc, dec over next 2 sc, sc in each of next 23 sc; dec over next 2 sc, sc in each of next 22 sc; dec over next 2 sc, sc in last sc = 50 sc.

Row 8: Ch 1, turn; sc in each of first 23 sc, (dec over next 2 sc) twice; sc in each of rem 23 sc = 48 sc. Finish off rust; join black.

Row 9: With black, ch 2, turn; dc in each of first 7 sc, hdc in next sc, sc in each sc to last 8 sts; hdc in next sc, dc in each of last 7 sc. Finish off, leaving approx 18″ sewing length.

Finishing

With overcast st, sew bottom seam with black; then sew heel and back seam with rust.

CUFF: Working on inside of stocking, join grey with a sl st at top edge at seam.

Rnd 1: Ch 1, sc in each of 44 sts around, join with a sl st in beg sc.

Rnd 2: Ch 1, do not turn; sc in same st as joining and in each rem sc around; join with a sl st in beg sc.

Rnd 3: Rep Rnd 2.

Rnd 4 (inc rnd): Ch 1, do not turn; work 2 sc in same st as joining; sc in each of next 10 sc, * 2 sc in next sc, sc in each of next 10 sc; rep from * twice more, join with a sl st in beg sc = 48 sc.

Rnds 5 and 6: Rep Rnd 2, twice. At end of Rnd 6, change to green in joining sl st. [**To change color: Insert hook in beg sc, drop grey (do not cut—will be used again later); hook green and pull through st and lp on hook = color changed**].

Rnd 7: With green, rep Rnd 2. At end of rnd, change to red (as before); finish off green.

Rnd 8: With red, rep Rnd 2. At end of rnd, change to grey; finish off red.

Rnd 9: With grey, rep Rnd 2.

Finish off; weave in ends. Fold down cuff.

LACE: With rust, sew one D-ring to each marked st at center front, having curved portion of rings facing center of stocking. Then lace red sport lace up front of stocking through rings and tie into a bow at top.

LOOP: With grey, ch 15, sl st in 15th ch from hook. Finish off, leaving approx 6″ sewing length. Sew loop to top center back of stocking.

KNITTED FISHERMAN CHRISTMAS STOCKING

designed by Mary Thomas

This beautiful heirloom stocking is knitted in the traditional off-white yarn, with interesting dimensional stitches. It may look complex, but it is really a pleasure to knit.

Size

Approx 6″ wide (*across top*) × 13″ long (*from folded edge of cuff to base of heel*).

Materials

Worsted weight yarn:
    4½ oz off white
Size 8, 10″ straight knitting needles (*or size required for gauge*)
Size 8, 7″ double pointed needles (*abbreviated dpn*)— or size required for gauge

Size 9, 10″ straight knitting needles (*for cuff only*)
Cable needle

Gauge

With smaller size needles, in stock st, 9 sts = 2″; 6 rows = 1″

Fisherman Pattern Stitches

LEFT BEADED RIB: (worked over 4 end sts)
Row 1 (wrong side): P2, K2.
Row 2: P2, K1, P1.

Rep Rows 1 and 2 for patt.

CENTER BEADED RIB: (worked over center 7 sts)
Row 1 (wrong side): K2, P3, K2.
Row 2: P2; K1, P1, K1; P2.

Rep Rows 1 and 2 for patt.

RIGHT BEADED RIB: (worked over 4 end sts)
Row 1 (wrong side): K2, P2.
Row 2: P1, K1, P2.

Rep Rows 1 and 2 for patt.

COIN CABLE: (worked over 9 sts)
Row 1 (wrong side): K2, P5, K2.
Row 2 (cable twist row): P2; sl next 4 sts onto cable needle and hold at **back** of work, K1; sl 3 sts from cable needle back onto left-hand needle (one st now on cable needle); bring cable needle to **front** of work (between knitting needles, keeping yarn to your right) and hold at **front** of work; K3, then K1 from cable needle; P2.
Rows 3 and 5: Rep Row 1.
Rows 4 and 6: P2, K5, P2.

Rep Rows 1 through 6 for patt.

NOSEGAY: (worked over 16 sts)
Row 1 (wrong side): K7, P2, K7.
Row 2: P6, work BKC (back knit cross) (**To work BKC: Sl next st onto cable needle and hold at back of work; K1, then K1 from cable needle = BKC**

made). Work FKC (front knit cross) (**To work FKC: Sl next st onto cable needle and hold at front of work; K1, then K1 from cable needle = FKC made**); P6.
Row 3: K5; work FC (front cross) (**To work FC: Sl next st onto cable needle and hold at front of work; P1, then K1 from cable needle = FC made**). P2; work BC (back cross) (**To work BC: Sl next st onto cable needle and hold at back of work; K1, then P1 from cable needle = BC made**); K5.
Row 4: P4, BC; BKC, FKC; FC, P4.
Row 5: K3, FC; K1, P4, K1; BC, K3.
Row 6: P2, BC, P1; BC, K2, FC; P1, FC, P2.
Row 7: (K2, P1) twice; K1, P2, K1; (P1, K2) twice.
Row 8: P2; work a bobble in next st [**To work bobble: Work (K1, P1) twice in next st; turn, P4; turn, K4; turn, (P2 tog) twice; turn, K2 tog = bobble made**). P1, BC; P1, K2, P1; FC, P1; work a bobble in next st, P2.
Row 9: K4, P1; K2, P2, K2; P1, K4.
Row 10: P4, work a bobble in next st; P2, K2, P2; work a bobble in next st, P4.

Rep Rows 1 through 10 for patt.

Instructions

Beg at cuff, with larger size straight needles, cast on 71 sts. Work in twisted rib patt as follows:

Row 1 (right side): Knit **in back lp** (*Fig 6*) of first st; * P1, knit **in back lp** of next st; rep from * across.

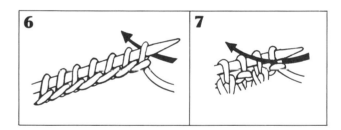

Row 2: Purl **in back lp** (*Fig 7*) of first st; * K1, purl **in back lp** of next st; rep from * across. Rep Rows 1 and 2 until cuff measures approx 1¾″ from cast-on edge. Change to smaller size straight needles and continue in twisted rib patt until cuff measures approx 4″ from cast-on edge, ending by working Row 1.

Next row (inc row): Continuing in twisted rib patt (Row 2), * work 5 sts, knit in front and back of next st (inc made); work 3 sts, inc; rep from * once more; work 7 sts, inc; work one st, inc; work 11 sts, inc; work one st, inc; work 7 sts, (inc, work 3 sts; inc, work 5 sts) twice = 83 sts. Now establish Fisherman Patt Sts.

Row 1 (wrong side of stocking—right side of cuff): Work Row 1 of each Patt St in the following sequence: Left Beaded Rib (4 sts); Coin Cable (9 sts); Nosegay (16 sts); Coin Cable (9 sts); Center Beaded Rib (7 sts); Coin Cable (9 sts); Nosegay (16 sts); Coin Cable (9 sts); Right Beaded Rib (4 sts).

Work even in patterns as established until 40 rows of

Fisherman Patt Sts have been completed. (*NOTE: You should now have a total of 4 repeats of Nosegay Patt.*)

Dec row (wrong side): Keeping patterns as established, work 4 sts, K2 tog; work 30 sts, K2 tog; work 7 sts, K2 tog; work 30 sts, K2 tog; work 4 rem sts = 79 sts.

Keeping continuity of patterns, work even for 9 more rows. (*NOTE: You should now have a total of 50 rows of Fisherman Patt Sts—5 repeats of Nosegay Patt.*)

Dec row (wrong side): Keeping patterns as established, work 3 sts, K2 tog; work 30 sts, K2 tog; work 5 sts, K2 tog; work 30 sts, K2 tog; work 3 rem sts = 75 sts.

Keeping continuity of patterns, work even for 9 more rows. (*NOTE: You should now have a total of 60 rows of Fisherman Patt Sts—6 repeats of Nosegay Patt.*)

Dec row (wrong side): P2, K2 tog; P5, K2 tog; K6, (K2 tog) twice; K8, P5; K2, P3, K2; P5, K8; (K2 tog) twice, K6, K2 tog, P5; K2 tog, P2 = 67 sts.

Next row (right side): P1, K1, P1; twist cable over next 5 sts, P 17; twist cable over next 5 sts, work next 7 sts in Center Beaded Rib Patt as established; twist cable over next 5 sts, P 17; twist cable over next 5 sts, P1, K1, P1.

Dividing row (wrong side): With dpn, sl first st as to purl, P 15 (16 sts now on one dpn for half of heel). With straight needle, K9, work next 17 sts in patterns as established (Coin Cable—5 sts; Center Beaded Rib—7 sts; Coin Cable—-5 sts); K9 (35 sts now on straight needle for instep). Sl rem 16 sts to 2nd dpn (for other half of heel).

INSTEP: Leaving 16 heel sts on each end on dpns (to be worked later), continue with smaller size straight needles and work instep on center 35 sts.

Row 1 (right side): K1, P8; work next 17 sts in patterns as established; P8, K1.

Row 2: K9, work next 17 sts in patterns as established, K9. Rep last 2 rows until instep measures approx 5″ long, ending by twisting cables on a right-side row. (*NOTE: You should now have 5 more repeats of Coin Cable Patt.*)

Dec row (wrong side): K9, P1; (P2 tog) twice, K2; P3, K2, P1; (P2 tog) twice, K9 = 31 sts.

Cut yarn, leaving approx 24″ sewing length. Leave sts on needle (to be worked later for toe).

HEEL: Hold stocking with right side facing you and heel sts on 2 dpns at top (outer edges of stocking will be in the center between dpns). Join yarn at left outer edge of stocking (between dpns) and knit sts from left dpn onto right dpn = 32 sts now on one dpn. Continue **with both dpns** and work back and forth in rows as follows:

Row 1 (wrong side): Sl 1 as to purl, purl rem sts.

Row 2: Sl 1 as to purl, knit rem sts.

Rep Rows 1 and 2, 7 times more. (*NOTE: You should now have a total of 16 rows, ending by working a knit row.*) Now turn heel.

TURN HEEL: (*NOTE: Heel is turned by working short rows; when instructions say "turn," leave rem sts unworked, turn work and begin next row.*)

Row 1 (wrong side): Sl 1 as to purl, P 20; P2 tog, P1, turn.

Row 2: Sl 1 as to purl, K 11; sl 1 as to knit, K1, PSSO; K1, turn.

Row 3: Sl 1 as to purl, P 12; P2 tog, P1, turn.

Row 4: Sl 1 as to purl, K 13; sl 1 as to knit, K1, PSSO; K1, turn.

Row 5: Sl 1 as to purl, P 14; P2 tog, P1, turn.

Row 6: Sl 1 as to purl, K 15; sl 1 as to knit, K1, PSSO; K1, turn.

Row 7: Sl 1 as to purl, P 16; P2 tog, P1, turn.

Row 8: Sl 1 as to purl, K 17; sl 1 as to knit, K1, PSSO; K1, turn.

Row 9: Sl 1 as to purl, P 18; P2 tog, P1, turn.

Row 10: Sl 1 as to purl, K 19; sl 1 as to knit, K1, PSSO; K1 = 22 sts.

Cut yarn, leaving sts on needle. Now work gusset and foot.

GUSSET AND FOOT: With right side of heel just made facing you, join yarn (leave approx 24″ sewing length) and **with free dpn**, pick up 10 sts along right edge of heel; K 22 (heel sts), then pick up 10 sts along left edge of heel = 42 sts. Continue **with 2 dpns** and work back and forth in rows.

Row 1 (wrong side): Purl.

Row 2: K1; sl 1 as to knit, K1, PSSO; knit to last 3 sts, K2 tog, K1 = 40 sts. Rep Rows 1 and 2, 4 times more = 32 sts. Continuing in stock st, work even until piece measures same length as instep, ending by working a knit row. Do not cut yarn; continue with dpns and work toe in rnds.

TOE: Joining rnd: Leave 32 sts just worked **on first dpn; with 2nd dpn**, K 15 from straight needle (instep); **with 3rd dpn**, knit rem 16 sts from straight needle = 63 sts. Join and continue shaping in rnds as follows:

Rnd 1: Knit.

Rnd 2 (First needle): K1; sl 1 as to knit, K1, PSSO; knit to last 3 sts, K2 tog, K1. **2nd needle:** K1; sl 1 as to knit, K1, PSSO; knit rem sts. **3rd needle:** Knit to last 3 sts, K2 tog, K1 = 59 sts. Rep Rnds 1 and 2 until 19 sts rem. Cut yarn, leaving approx 12″ end. Thread into tapestry or yarn needle and weave through rem sts twice (removing knitting needles). Draw up tightly and fasten securely. Weaven in all yarn ends. Weave seams tog. Fold down half of ribbing for cuff.

LOOP: With smaller size straight needles, cast on 3 sts.

Row 1 (right side): K1, P1, K1.

Row 2: Purl. Rep Rows 1 and 2 until piece measures approx 4″ long. Bind off, leaving approx 6″ sewing length. Fold in half, having wrong sides tog. Sew ends to top of stocking at seam.

CANDLEWICKING

Candlewicking! The very name conjures up the picture of our Colonial ancestor saving her tiny bits of candlewick thread, left over from her day's candlemaking, and from these bits creating beautiful counterpanes. It sounds very romantic, but probably isn't true. Candlewicking probably developed first among the very wealthy; the finest surviving examples of early Candlewicking are in restored manor houses, such as Mount Vernon. Candlewicking was done on huge looms by servants, using a soft spun cotton thread, called "wicking" or "candlewicking."

Whether done by hand or on a loom, Candlewicking was traditionally created in one of two ways. In the first method a row of evenly spaced running stitches was made. Several strands of thread were used to give results of varying size. The strands were cut halfway between the stitches, resulting in tufts. After washing in very hot water, the fabric shrunk, and the tufts stood up. Rubbing the tufts with a brush before they were completely dry helped in fluffing them up. A little shaking completed the fluffing process; Candlewicking then and now is never ironed! If the stitches had been worked close together, the tufts were a solid mass; if the stitches were farther apart, the tufts made a dotted line. In the second method, the thread was laid on top of the fabric. Then a sewing thread was used to tack down (or couch) the strands in place. Again the strands were cut with a sharp-pointed scissors between the stitches, and the washing caused the fabric to shrink and the tufts to stand up.

These methods of Candlewicking were used as late as the first half of the twentieth century. In addition, machines were invented to do the work. The results were thousands of "chenille" bedspreads and bathrobes, which gave the effect of Candlewicking without the work.

Now with the renewed interest in our heritage, the art of Candlewicking has returned. But the old methods seem too rigid and slow for our modern pace, and modern technology has left us with fabrics that barely shrink and threads that no longer fluff. Never mind! We can still produce beautiful examples of this old art. We no longer have to tack our wicking down on the fabric and then cut it to create puffs. We simply use French and colonial knots to create beautiful designs. (In addition, there is a heritage of using French and Colonial knots in Candlewicking. Many early examples of this craft have huge knots worked alongside the traditional methods in the design.) We can create the other effects of Candlewicking with Stem and Outline Stitch, Padded Satin and by Couching. We use the hot water bath to shrink the fabric just slightly so that it produces the soft wrinkled look of old-time Candlewicking. Our new form of Candlewicking is following our American tradition, for nothing could be more traditionally American than to keep the best of the old, but ever translating traditions into new, easy-to-do ways. That is called progress.

CANDLEWICKING HOW-TO

THE FABRIC

Candlewicking is usually done on 100% cotton un-bleached muslin, which has *not* been pre-shrunk. Do not wash this fabric before stitching on it. The fabric is washed after stitching; the shrinkage will not only hold the knots, but it will also give the project the puckered look of traditional Candlewicking. If you prefer less shrinkage, purchase a good quality 100% cotton, which will shrink only about 2% to 3%. If you like the puckered look, buy a fabric which will give you an 8% to 10% shrinkage. All of our Christmas projects were made on fabric with a minimum of shrinkage. Traditionally, Candlewicking was stitched white on white; but today various colored threads are being used.

THE THREAD

Our ornaments were made with special Candlewicking thread, which is 100% cotton and has four plies. The plies can be separated and used in different combinations. If Candlewicking thread is not available, you can substitute other threads, such as crochet cotton, embroidery floss, pearl cotton, cotton knit and crochet yarn, darning yarn—even kite twine. Because threads do differ in thickness, experiment until you achieve the desired effect. You may use only one strand, or more than 20, depending on the individual thread.

THE NEEDLES

You'll need a sharp, long-eyed needle, such as a #2 Crewel Needle or a #20 Chenille Needle. Or look for a newly available packet of needles called "Candlewicking Assortment."

THE HOOPS

Stretch the fabric in an embroidery hoop or small quilting frame. Keep the fabric taut for easier stitching.

STITCHING

Traditional embroidery stitches—French Knots, Stem/Outline, Padded Satin are used in our blocks. One stitch that may be new to you is the Colonial Knot, which is a simple variation of the French Knot. All of the stitches, except the Colonial Knot, are worked with 2 strands of Candlewicking thread. We suggest you cut the thread twice the stitching length desired (about 36"), thread it into the needle, bring ends together and make a knot. This gives you an 18" stitching length. Working this way, rather than using 2 individual 18" strands, gives an even tension and, because there is less bulk near the eye, makes it easier to pull the thread through fabric.

The Colonial Knot is worked with 4 strands. Cut 2 strands about 36" long, and thread into needle. Bring all 4 ends together and knot. Candlewicking is one of the few embroidery techniques in which knots should be used to start a new thread. To end off, run the needle back through an inch or so of stitching.

To keep the embroidery hoop from crushing the French and Colonial Knots, stitch them last. You can begin stitching in any area of the design, but avoid long jumps from one area to another; the thread across the back of the work will leave shadows.

Following are instructions for working stitches used in Candlewicking.

STEM/OUTLINE (worked with 2 strands): The needle comes up through work at 1 and all odd numbers, down through fabric at 2 and all even numbers. Keep thread below needle at all times. At point 5, bring needle up and from now on, always bring needle up through a previously used hole. Continue in this manner (*Fig 1*).

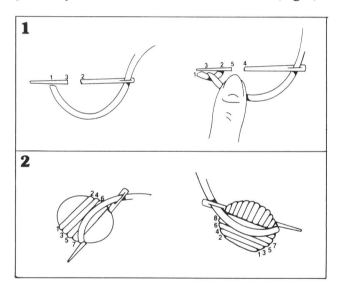

PADDED SATIN (worked with 2 strands): To give added dimension to the stitch, the traditional Satin Stitch is worked over a foundation of padding stitches. First work the padding, taking long stitches within the area outline, placed so they slant in the opposite direction in which the top Satin Stitches will go. Bring needle up at 1 and all odd stitches, down at 2 and all even stitches (*Fig 2*).

FRENCH KNOTS (worked with 2 strands): Bring needle up at 1, hold thread close to work with left thumb and index finger. Slip needle under thread, and turn needle clockwise. Still holding thread in left fingers, insert needle back down through fabric at 2, maintaining firm tension on thread until it is almost completely down through the fabric (*Fig 3*).

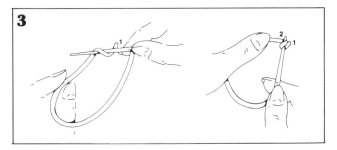

COLONIAL KNOTS (worked with 4 strands): Step 1: Bring needle up through fabric at 1, then hold thread firmly with left thumb and index finger about 2″ from point 1. Hold threaded needle in right hand as you would hold a pencil and cross over left hand so needle goes *under* the thread from *left* side (*Fig 4*). This is an awkward step and does take some practice before it becomes a comfortable and natural movement. Note figure showing the wrong way.

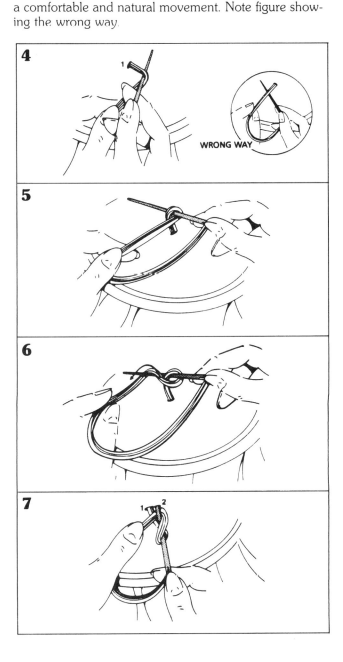

WRONG WAY

Step 2: Continue to hold thread firmly with left thumb and index finger and turn needle to left (from vertical to horizontal position), which loops thread around needle (*Fig 5*).

Step 3: With left hand bring thread up and over needle (*Fig 6*). The thread now forms a figure 8.

Step 4: Turn needle back to vertical position and insert it down through fabric at 2. Continuing to hold thread firmly with left hand, pull needle and thread down through fabric, giving left hand thread a firm tug just before thread is pulled completely through (*Fig 7*). This assures a tight, firm knot.

HOW TO TRANSFER THE DESIGNS

Step 1: Do not wash the fabric. Unless otherwise specified, always cut a larger piece than required for the project. This extra fabric will make it easier to embroider.

Step 2: Iron the fabric so that it is smooth.

Step 3: Open book to desired pattern and lay book flat. A piece of white paper or cardboard placed under page will be a help in seeing pattern clearly.

Step 4: Lay fabric over design and tape down.

Step 5: With water-soluble marking pen, trace pattern. The broken lines around the design indicates **sewing** line. Be sure to trace sewing line. (*NOTE: Test all water-soluble pens before using to make absolutely sure that dots will wash out.*). Never trust manufacturers' statements. The dots should wash out cleanly without leaving any residue on fabric or thread.

CANDLEWICKING THE DESIGNS

The stitch charts show what stitches we used in our projects. Feel free to substitute stitches as you choose; if we show an area worked with Padded Satin, you might prefer to fill it with Colonial Knots, or leave it open and work Stem/Outline around it.

WASHING THE CANDLEWICKING

In traditional Candlewicking, washing the completed embroidery in very hot water was the final step. This caused the fabric to shrink, and the stitches to stand up. Today, the hot water bath will cause the fabric to shrink slightly, giving the work the soft, puckered look of antique Candlewicking.

Before attempting the hot water bath, wash Candlewicking in cold water to remove all traces of marking pen. Make sure that there are no blue lines hiding in fabric to haunt you later. If fabric is very soiled, you may wish to use a mild soap.

Now wash your Candlewicking in very hot water to cause the fabric to shrink as described above. Roll fabric in soft terry towel to eliminate moisture. Unroll and place stitched piece face down on a dry terry towel on ironing board and steam until dry. This will make embroidery "stand up". Do not let the steam iron rest on the stitches; the steam does the work!

CANDLEWICK CHRISTMAS TREE ORNAMENTS

designed by Gretchen Wilhelm

Make one or all of the delightful Candlewick ornaments to add a special charm to your Christmas tree. Our materials make all three ornaments. If you wish to place the Candlewick designs on both sides of the ornament, double the thread requirement.

Size

4″ high

Materials

½ yd Candlewicking fabric
15 yds Candlewicking thread
Polyester fiberfill

Instructions

Step 1: Cut a piece of Candlewick fabric 10″ × 10″ for each design. Following above instructions, trace the design. With your water soluble marking pen, also mark the sewing line.

Step 2: Candlewick the fabric. Before washing in cold water to remove blue Candlewicking markings, baste (or stay stitch on your sewing machine) around the sewing line. (*NOTE: Once you wash the fabric in cold water, sewing lines will disappear.*)

Step 3: Following the instructions on page 135, wash the fabric in cold and hot water.

Step 4: Cut a piece of Candlewicking fabric for the backing the same size as the embroidered piece.

Step 5: Right sides together, join the two pieces sewing along the previously marked sewing line. Sew all around, leaving a large enough opening for turning.

Step 6: Cut ¼″ around the sewing line, clipping where necessary to maintain the shape. Turn ornament right side out.

Step 7: Stuff with polyester fiberfill. Slip stitch the opening.

Step 8: Attach loop for hanging.

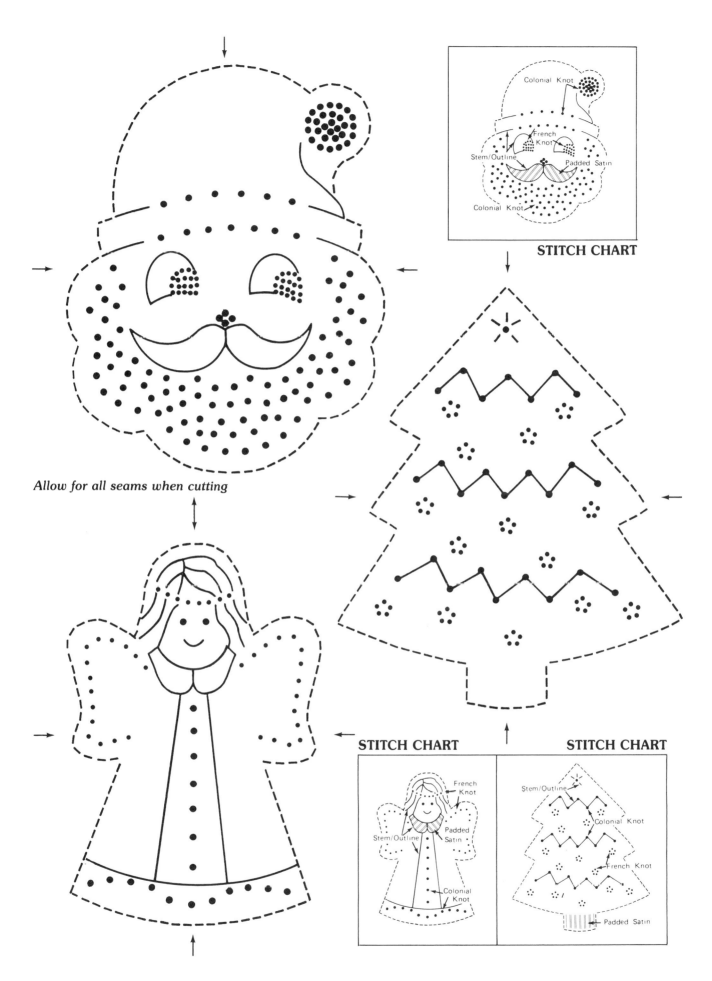

Allow for all seams when cutting

STITCH CHART

STITCH CHART

STITCH CHART

137

CANDLEWICK SNOWFLAKES

designed by Rita Weiss and Gretchen Wilhelm

Make some or all of these delightful snowflakes and hang them on your tree or use them to decorate your house. We show them made with white candlewick thread on a pale blue 100% cotton. You might prefer to make them in the traditional white on white.

Size

3″ in diameter

Materials

(for each snowflake)
Two 8″ × 8″ pieces pale blue 100% cotton fabric
5 yds natural Candlewicking thread
⅓ yd pre-gathered lace trimming
8″ × 8″ piece quilt batting

Instructions

Step 1: Following the instructions on page 135, trace one of the designs on pages 139, 140. With your water soluble pen, also mark the sewing line. Trace two designs for each snowflake—one for the back and one for the front.

Step 2: Candlewick the fabric. Before washing in cold water to remove markings, run a row of stitches around the sewing line. *NOTE: Once you wash the fabric in cold water, sewing lines will disappear.*

Step 3: Following instructions, wash fabric in cold and hot water.

Step 4: Right sides together and raw edges even, baste the trimming in place on the right side of one of the candlewicked snowflakes.

Step 5: Lay the square of quilt batting on a flat surface and cover with the snowflake that has no trimming, right side up. Lay the snowflake with the trimming on the first snowflake, wrong side up. Pin or baste carefully. *NOTE: If you are joining by machine, you must place tissue paper under the batting so that the batting will not get caught as you work. Tear the tissue paper away when you have finished joining the seams.*

Step 6: Stitch around the outer edges, leaving an opening wide enough for turning.

Step 7: Carefully cut approximately ¼″ around the sewing line, clipping where necessary to maintain the shape.

Step 8: Turn snowflake right side out, and push into corners with a blunt pencil or similar tool. Slip stitch the opening and attach a loop for hanging.

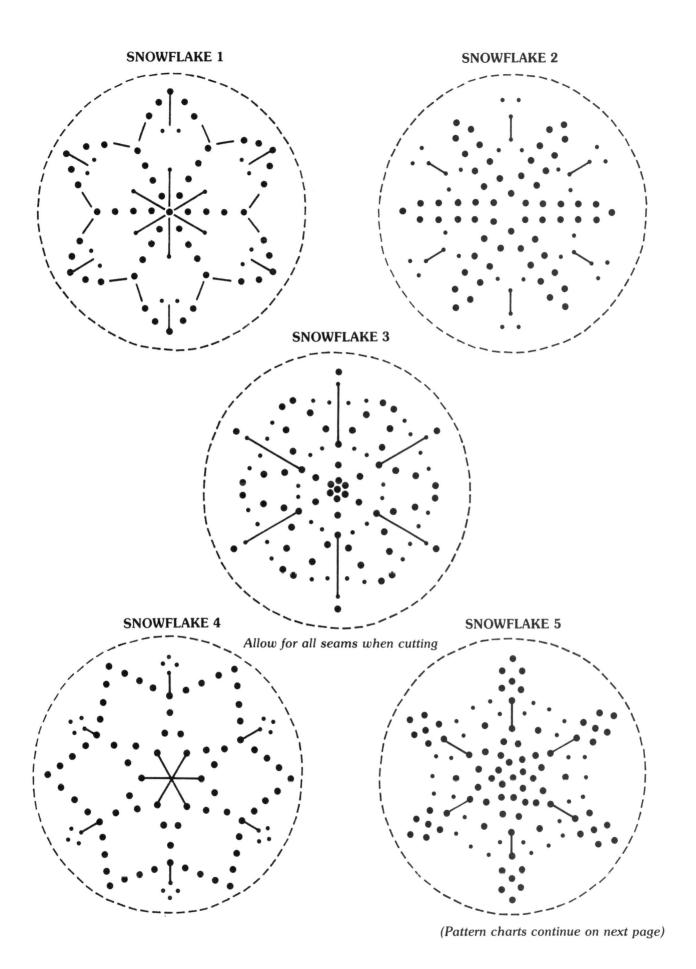

SNOWFLAKE 1

SNOWFLAKE 2

SNOWFLAKE 3

Allow for all seams when cutting

SNOWFLAKE 4

SNOWFLAKE 5

(Pattern charts continue on next page)

SNOWFLAKE 6   SNOWFLAKE 7

Allow for all seams when cutting

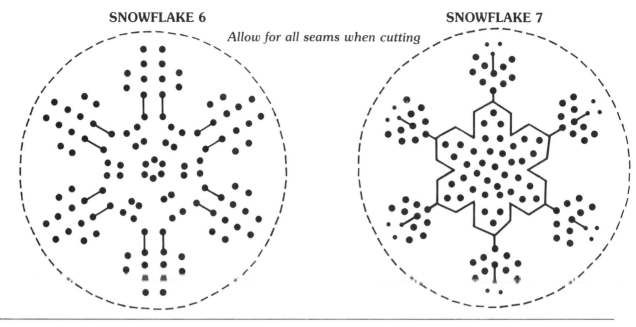

SNOWFLAKE STITCH CHARTS

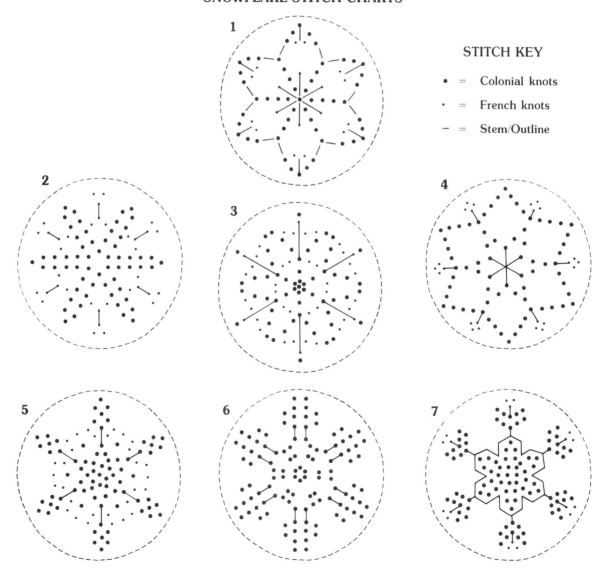

STITCH KEY

● = Colonial knots

· = French knots

− = Stem/Outline

140

CANDLEWICK MINI CHRISTMAS WREATHS

designed by Rita Weiss and Gretchen Wilhelm

Use the same Candlewick designs that were used for the snowflakes, but embroider them with colored Candlewick thread, frame them in embroidery hoops—and you create our mini Christmas wreaths.

Size

3″ in diameter

Materials

(for each mini-wreath)
Two 8″ × 8″ pieces Candlewick fabric
5 yds colored Candlewicking thread (*we used red, green and gold*)
⅓ yd pre-gathered lace trimming
3″ wooden embroidery hoop
8″ × 8″ piece quilt batting (*optional*)
8″ × 8″ piece white felt (*optional*)
Ribbon (*optional*)

Instructions

Step 1: Following instructions, trace one of the designs on pages 139, 140. It is not necessary to trace the sewing line.

Step 2: Candlewick the fabric.

Step 3: Following above instructions, wash fabric in cold and hot water.

Step 4: Place stitched piece wrong side up on a flat surface, and center outer ring of hoop over design. With a pencil lightly draw around hoop. Measure and draw a 1″ allowance all around circle. Remove hoop, pin stitched piece to unstitched fabric, and then cut out both fabrics at same time along allowance line. (*NOTE: You may, if you wish, add a thin layer of batting to be sandwiched between the Candlewick piece and the backing.*)

Step 5: If you wish, you can paint the hoop, using regular acrylic paint. Paint only the outer ring. You will probably need to apply one coat, let it dry, then a second coat. Be sure paint is completely dry before proceeding. Do not paint metal screw.

Step 6: Place inner ring of hoop on flat surface. Place stitched piece and backing (and batting, if desired) together on top of inner ring, and center design carefully. Place outer ring on top of fabric, slide down over inner ring. Adjust screw to hold work taut, pulling fabric as necessary to eliminate wrinkles.

Step 7: Turn project to back side; with needle and sewing thread, run a gathering line through all fabric layers around outer edge of work, about ¼″ in from outer fabric edge. Pull up gathers so work lies flat in back. Secure thread firmly. Glue ruffle to back of hoop. If desired, a felt circle can be glued to back of piece to hide gathered area.

Step 8: Tie a ribbon bow on metal ring, if desired. Attach loop for hanging.

CANDLEWICK
TREE-TOP ANGELS

designed by Rita Weiss and Gretchen Wilhelm

What could be more elegant than a white-on-white Candlewick angel on your tree. We give you your choice of two versions: an angel with a candle and an angel with a trumpet.

Size

5¾" high

Materials
(for each angel)

Two 10" × 10" pieces Candlewicking fabric
8 yds natural Candlewicking thread
10" × 10" piece quilt batting

Instructions

Step 1: Following instructions, trace design. With water soluble pen, also mark the sewing line.

Step 2: Candlewick the fabric. Before washing in cold water to remove markings, run a row of stitches around the sewing line. *NOTE: Once you wash fabric in cold water, sewing lines will disappear.*

Step 3: Following instructions, wash fabric in cold and hot water. Iron.

Step 4: Cut a piece of Candlewicking fabric for the backing which is the same size as the Candlewicked piece. Or, if you prefer, make two Candlewicked pieces, one for the back and one for the front.

Step 5: Lay a square of quilt batting—slightly larger than the Candlewicked piece—on a flat surface and cover with the backing fabric, right side up. Lay the Candle-

wicked piece on the backing fabric, wrong side up. Pin or baste carefully. *NOTE: If you are joining by machine, you must place tissue paper under the batting so that the batting does not get caught as you work. Tear the tissue paper away when you have finished joining the seam.*

Step 6: Stitch around the outer edges, leaving an opening wide enough for turning. Carefully cut approximately ¼" around the sewing line, clipping where necessary to maintain shape. Turn ornament right side out and push into corners with blunt pencil or similar tool.

Step 7: Slip stitch the opening, and attach loop for hanging.

Step 8: If you wish to add definition to the design, quilt around the body of the angel as we have done.

STITCH CHART

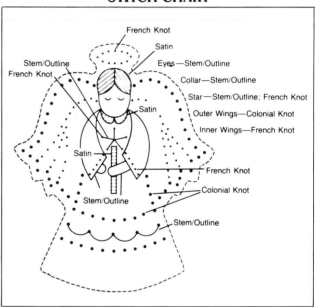

STITCH CHART

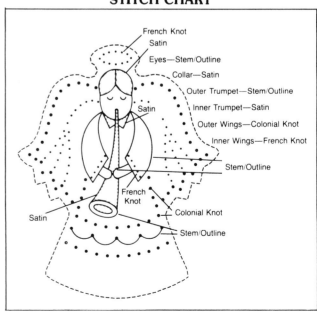

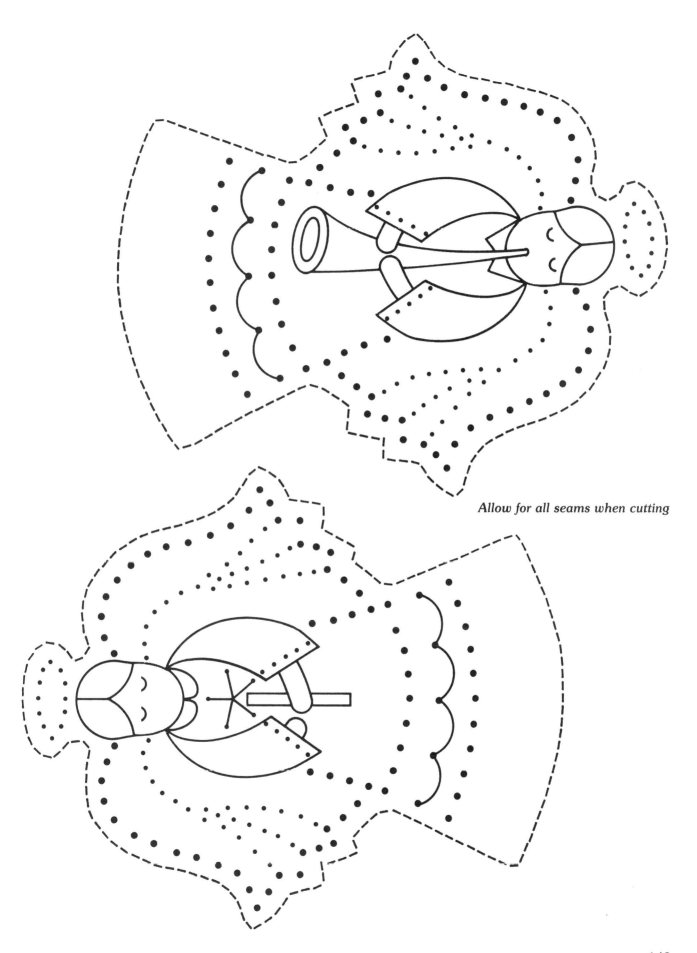

Allow for all seams when cutting

143

Index

Angel
    Candlewick, 137, 142–143
    Crochet, 113–114
    Cross Stitch, 96
Argyle Stocking, 127–129

Candlewicking, 134–143
Centerpiece, Plastic Canvas, 46, 51, 54
Church, Plastic Canvas, 61
Coaster, Plastic Canvas, 37
Cottage, Plastic Canvas, 46
Counted Cross Stitch, 82–104
Crocheting and Knitting, 106–132

Fisherman Knit Stocking, 130

Gift Box, Plastic Canvas, 40–41

Houses, Plastic Canvas, 42–50, 61–64
How-To
    Candlewicking, 134–135
    Crocheting, 106–109
    Cross Stitch, 82–85
    Knitting, 109–112
    Patchwork, 8–10
    Plastic Canvas, 34–36
    Pompons, 28–29
    Quilting, 10

Knitting and Crocheting, 106–132

Log Cabin, Plastic Canvas, 42

Napkin, 20
    Ring, Plastic Canvas, 37, 54
Nativity, Cross Stitch, 87–90, 100–103
Needlepoint, Plastic Canvas, 34–64

Ornaments
    Candlewick, 136–137
    Crochet, 119–120
    Cross Stitch, 96, 104

Package Decorations, 30, 115
Patchwork, 8–26
Pillows, Patchwork, 13–18
Placemats
    Patchwork, 19–20
    Plastic Canvas, 37, 54
Plastic Canvas Needlepoint, 34–64
Pompons, 28–32

Quilting, 10

Santa
    Candlewick, 137
    Cross Stitch, 104
    Plastic Canvas, 51, 104
    Pompons, 30
Sleigh, Plastic Canvas, 54
Snowflakes
    Candlewick, 138–140
    Crochet, 117–118
Stockings
    Crochet, 116, 125–127, 129–130
    Cross Stitch, 91–93

Knit, 115, 127–129, 130–135
    Patchwork, 23–24
Stitches
    Back, 84
    Binding, 36
    Colonial Knots, 135
    Compensating, 36
    Continental, 35
    Cross, 83
    French Knots, 84, 134
    Half Cross, 35
    Overcast, 36
    Satin, Padded, 134
    Stem/Outline, 134
    Tacking, 36

Templates, 8, 11–12
Tote Bag, Patchwork, 21–22
Tree-Top Angel
    Candlewick, 142–143
    Crochet, 113–114
Tree
    Candlewick, 137
    Crochet, 121–123, 123–124
    Cross Stitch, 94–95
    Pompon, 31–32
Tree Skirt, Patchwork, 25–26
Trunk, Plastic Canvas, 40

Wall Hanging, Cross Stitch, 97
Wreath
    Candlewick, 141
    Crochet, 123–124